An Evening in Chicago
Published by The University Club of Chicago Writing Society.
76 E. Monroe Street, Chicago, IL 60603

ISBN-13: 978-1503183841

Introduction

An evening in Chicago among its 2.7 million inhabitants yields many stories – of love, lust, crime, tragedy, death, disillusionment, birth, fortune, reconciliation, revelation, and hope.

While these themes will be familiar to readers, many of the short stories in *An Evening in Chicago* will introduce them to colorful characters and unusual circumstances outside the realm of everyday experience. All of these stories are set among the soaring skyline, beloved landmarks, colorful neighborhoods, and great lake that define Chicago.

Written by the members of the University Club of Chicago Writing Society, these stories will enrich readers' insights into the city and its people and forever change their perspective of what can happen when the sun sets over Chicago.

The University Club of Chicago Writing Society, December 2014

MARK BACHARACH	SID MITCHELL
ED BACHRACH	BARBARA PERRY
SALLY CAMPBELL	MICHAEL K. POLLARD
MARY ERHARD	ROXANA SULLIVAN
ALLYSON LANG	BILL TRUDE
SCOTT MCGARVEY	KAREN EBERT YANCEY
ROSE MCINERNEY	GREGORY ZAYIA

Table of Contents

Photo: Lina Grigaitis. Afghans: Mary Bonadonna.

Gregory Zayia is an organic chemist, violinist, and patent agent. He is the editor of Maestro Ruggiero Ricci's treatise on violin playing, Ricci on Glissando: The Shortcut to Violin Technique *(Indiana University Press, 2007), and is presently editing the legendary violinist's memoirs. Gregory lives in Chicago with his wife, Lina Grigaitis, and their children, Adriana, Christopher, and Angelina.*

No Deadlines

By Gregory Zayia

CORA SACHTER PEERED DOWN OVER the tawny, scratched lenses of her Woolworth reading glasses, searching the zigzags of her latest afghan – a midnight blue and turquoise bedspread – for the stitch she had dropped sometime during the past hour. She had continued to knit, vaguely conscious of the dropped stitch, and now, once she tracked it down, she would have to rip several rows of work and redo them. *Should have stopped right away,* she thought. But the steady clicking of her knitting needles had soothed her, and it took her mind off things, sitting in Gerhard's favorite armchair, knitting in time to the gentle tick-tock of the cuckoo clock.

She found the dropped stitch and sighed, then slipped her needles out of the loops and placed them in the wicker basket alongside her chair. Gerhard's colleagues at the university had sent her the fruit basket along with a sympathy card signed by the entire chemistry faculty the morning after his fatal stroke. Two weeks later, when she dumped the rotting fruit into the garbage, she had decided to keep the empty basket to store her knitting needles and loose skeins of yarn. And for close to eleven years, the basket had sat on the hardwood floor, always within an arm's reach of Gerhard's favorite chair.

Cora tugged at a strand of blue yarn and started to unravel the work of the past hour. She thought about her best friend Birdie McPherson, and how Thursdays and Sundays, before Birdie died last April, she used to ride the bus to Cora's apartment and spend her afternoon knitting and chatting, right alongside Cora in the matching tweed armchair. Cora glanced at the empty chair to her right, then down again at the curled strand of blue yarn piling up on her lap. *Three rows of work wasted,* she thought. Birdie could never understand Cora's perfectionism. "So you dropped a stitch. Who's going to know?" Birdie would say. Cora smiled, remembering how Birdie dropped stitch after stitch, sometimes even switched patterns right in the middle of an afghan without even realizing. But Birdie never once ripped a single line of work after it was finished. It wasn't her age – Cora had known Birdie for over thirty years, and even before the Alzheimer's, Birdie had always done sloppy work.

Cora was quite proud of her own afghans – and her sweaters, scarves, winter caps, baby blankets. Her standards were uncompromising and her work always of the finest quality. Yet what did it matter? At least Birdie's sons, and her grandchildren – even her daughters-in-law – at least *they* appreciated the old lady's efforts. They always used to send Birdie thank-you cards for her gifts – sweaters that didn't fit, bedspreads too short for the beds they were supposed to cover. And sometimes they even invited her over for dinner – just *something* to show their gratitude. *It's nice to have family close,* Cora thought.

Why did she even bother with the baby blankets? Two grown sons – two *married* grown sons – but no grandchildren. Still, it passed the time and soon, after she finished six more rows (assuming she didn't drop another stitch), she would be finished with yet another afghan. A sturdy white cardboard box from Woolworth's – the same type of box she used to store all her work – lay on the bed, already assembled, and as soon as she finished these last six rows, she would arrange the afghan neatly in the box and stack it atop a dozen others inside the hall closet.

Dr. Braverman had told Cora not to get overly excited – they had detected her cancer quite early, before it had much of a chance to spread, and there was an excellent chance that radiation treatments would be effective. Still, he admitted, the pancreas was just a bit tricky, and since she was up in years she might at least consider moving closer to one of her sons – just in case. Two days ago, Saturday morning, she had called Neville in New York. He was the oldest child and had inherited Gerhard's capacity for cool, dispassionate reasoning in times of crisis – not that she considered this a crisis. But her children usually called *her,* two, maybe three times a month, and Neville had been surprised to hear from her.

"Mom! What a surprise. How are you? Nothing's wrong, is it?"

"No, no," she said. "I'm just calling, nothing's wrong."

"Then why didn't you call collect? You should always call us collect. You shouldn't have to pay for this."

"And neither should you," Cora said. "Besides, it's not much."

She paused for a second and straightened out the names in her head. Daiva was the Lithuanian – Neville's wife – and Claudia was Dean's wife – yes, that was it. "How are you and Daiva?" she said.

"We're doing just fine, Mom. And how about you? Something's wrong, isn't it? I've got a feeling."

"Honestly," she said, "there's nothing wrong. I just wanted to ask your opinion about something."

"Anything," he said.

Well, how to put it? She thought. "I was thinking…" Her voice trailed off.

"You were thinking…"

"I've been thinking maybe about leaving Chicago…"

"Leaving Chicago?! Whoa, wait a second! You're kidding, right?"

"…leaving Chicago and moving closer to you or Dean…maybe moving to New York…but I wanted to get your opinion first."

"Wait a second, hold on, just wait a second now and let me sort this out. You're saying you want to leave Chicago?" His voice sounded strained, frightened, and he was talking fast. "Mom, don't get me wrong, we'd *love* to have you live closer, that wouldn't be a problem, in fact you could come and live with us if you *really* wanted to – that wouldn't be the problem – but…you're seventy-eight years old…"

"Seventy-seven," she corrected. "And I didn't mean come and live *with* you."

"All right, seventy-seven, and I'm not sure that moving *now* would be such a great plan. Do you have any idea what a change that would be for you? I mean, living independently like you do now, holding down the fort there in the Windy City, that's what keeps you going, that's what keeps you so fit, so *young.*" After a long pause, he said shortly: "You asked me for my opinion."

Then and there, Cora decided not to mention the cancer. This just wasn't the time. She didn't want to frighten him or make him feel guilty. She had merely wanted to sound him out, know his opinion – and now she had it.

"Mom?" he said.

"I'm here."

"First of all, *why?* Why would you even think of moving? After what is it – fifty years? You love Chicago. It's in your blood. Is there some reason? You're not sick or something, are you?"

"No, it's not that," she said, then paused. "I don't know, Neville. It was just an idea I had, but you're right – it *would* be hard to leave."

"You know we'd love to have you – *if* it were possible. And there's another thing – I never mention it because I know you'd worry – but New York is just not the safest city anymore. It's like a war zone here sometimes. Half the time, *I'm* frightened, and I just wouldn't feel right knowing you had to deal with it too. For starters, you wouldn't be able to walk around on your own, walk to the store, even go outside to get some fresh air. You wouldn't be able to do things here by yourself. I'd be constantly worried about you getting mugged or even worse."

How's the Upper East Side worse than the south side of Chicago? Cora thought.

"And your friends," he said. "What about your friends? What about that woman you knit with – what's her name?"

"Birdie?" she said.

"Birdie. What about Birdie? She'd be devastated if you left. And so would you. The people are not that friendly here, Mom."

"That's true," Cora said. "I hadn't thought about that. No, you're right, Neville. Absolutely right. That's why I wanted to get your opinion. See what you thought."

"I'm glad you did. But now I'm worried. What made you even bring this up? You didn't have some kind of premonition or something, did you?"

"A premonition?"

"Yes, a premonition. You know, like a bad feeling. You're okay, aren't you?

"Of course," she said.

"And you're keeping busy? With your knitting?"

"I'm working on a new afghan, a blue one. I think I can finish it by Monday."

"That's great!" he said. "Take your time, though. You don't have any deadlines to meet. God, I wish I could say that."

"Would you like it?" she said, "When I'm done? You and Claudia?"

"Claudia?"

Damn it! Why can't I keep those two straight? "I'm sorry, Daiva, you and Daiva. I think it would fit your bed. It's a nice, big king-size."

"Mom, that's really sweet! We couldn't though, not after all that work. You already made us one, remember? The one with the granny squares? It's on the bed in the spare room as we speak. We love it!"

That was almost ten years ago! she thought.

"We couldn't take another one, but thanks just the same. I bet it's beautiful. You know, you should consider selling one sometime. People would pay good money for those blankets. You'd be surprised."

SHE HAD CALLED NEVILLE ON SATURDAY, and he had promised to call her sometime during the week, to make sure things were okay. They didn't want the afghan, that's what he had said. So, in a few more hours, it would join the others in the hall closet. Dean and Claudia might like it, but they had only a double bed. Still, she had that purple and white double-sized she had finished last year. Canada was supposed to be cold, and even though they already had one, the one she had given them as a wedding gift, maybe they needed another one by now. *When he calls I'll ask him,* she thought.

Cora finished ripping the last row of yarn, tied a loose knot in the strand to mark her place, then plopped the heavy afghan onto the floor next to her chair. Why did she still work with such dark colors? They were hard on her eyes, and sometimes she dropped a stitch – like today. But ninety-nine cents had been such a good price, so she had bought twelve skeins of the midnight blue and twelve skeins of the turquoise – enough for a king-sized bedspread. She might have a skein or two of each left over, but she could always return them at the Woolworth, or exchange them for different colors – lighter colors.

Cuckoo! Cuckoo! Cuckoo! Cuckoo! Cora glanced up to her left at the clock on the wall. Four o'clock. The mustachioed wooden man in striped yellow pants waited patiently until the cuckoo disappeared behind its door, then stiffly turned the wheel of his hurdy-gurdy, grinding out the tinkling notes of an old Bavarian melody. She would take a little nap, rest her eyes a while, and then, after she made something to eat, finish these last few rows of the afghan. There was the stew and cabbage from last night – she could always warm that up – or maybe boil a package of rice medley for a change of pace. Cora closed her eyes and put up her feet on the embroidered footstool in front of the chair. *This is the last time I work with dark colors,* she decided.

Cora dreamed of their childhood, of Austria, of a winding cobblestone road, in Salzburg – or was it Grossgmain? She had been chasing Gerhard, laughing and breathless, past cafés, past storefronts, pleading with him to stop. When he did, he would face her just for a moment, his cheeks tinged red with the sting of Alpine wind, then spin around and race off again, laughing, just as she lunged to embrace him. At first she did not hear the knocks, tentative at first and then louder, but as they seeped into her consciousness they melted into the cadence of footsteps pounding across cobblestones.

When the knocks ceased, Cora woke with a start. She had slept longer than she had intended, and her mouth felt dry and pasty. The sitting room was dark now except for a few slivers of moonlight creeping through the window in back of her chair. At the other end of the apartment, through the narrow window over the kitchen sink, she saw that the street lamps had already been turned on.

A floorboard squeaked outside the hall door. Had someone been knocking? Cora lowered her feet from the footstool and straightened up in the chair, staring at the door and listening for more knocks. She heard silence, broken only by her breathing and the rhythmic tick-tock of the cuckoo clock. She glanced up. It was almost seven. Then she heard a slow creak, back and forth, like the sound of planks stretching deep in the keel of a wooden ship. The sound was coming from the doorjamb, her doorjamb. Had she locked the deadbolt? No, she mustn't have. She always locked it after dinner, right before getting ready for bed, but she hadn't eaten dinner tonight, had she? There was another long, grating creak, followed by the crisp snap of splintered wood. The door inched forward and the doorknob rattled.

Cora sat motionless, clutching the arms of the chair with her palms. *Was she still dreaming?* A dull, heavy thump, then another one, and the door flew inward, stopping with a bang when the brass knob bit into the plaster wall. Silhouetted against the dim light from the bulb in the hallway, Cora saw a thin, sandy-haired man – just a boy really – gripping a tire iron in one hand, an enormous canvas knapsack dangling limply from the other. *Why, he can't be twenty years old!* The man slid into the room, set the knapsack against the wall and pushed the door closed, leaning against it with his back and breathing quickly. His dark blue corduroys were too tight and too short, and she saw that his worn flannel shirt was missing a button at the bottom, so that it flapped open at his waist. He stood there leaning against the door for a full minute until, gradually, his breathing slowed and he stepped into the sitting room, opening his eyes for the first time.

He looked to the right, off into the kitchen, then to the left, at the window behind the armchairs. As his eyes adjusted to the dark, he noticed Cora, seated bolt upright in her chair, staring at him with wide eyes.

"Mother*fucker!*" he screamed, and thrust the tire iron out in front of him toward Cora, brandishing it from side to side like a sword. "Fuck!" he said viciously, then furrowed his brow, thinking. "All right, Lady, look…" He stroked the back of his neck, searching the floor with desperate eyes. "You alone?" he said at last.

Cora nodded.

"Anyone else live here?"

Cora shook her head and swallowed hard.

"That's good," he said. "All right, now look – "

Just then, the cuckoo darted through his arched green door and shrilly began to call the hour. *Cuckoo! Cuck –*

"Mother – " cried the man, spinning sideways towards the sound and stabbing at the air with his tire iron, and then his voice trailed off. "Oh," he said softly, then turned once again to Cora, waiting for the cuckoo to cease its chatter, and then for the last tinkles of the organ grinder's hurdy-gurdy to die away. "Okay, Lady, now look…"

Up until now, Cora had not fully grasped the significance of the situation, but the familiar voice of the cuckoo stirred her paralyzed thoughts into life. She had been sleeping, yes, she had dreamt of Austria and of Gerhard – but this was not part of the dream. No, this was real. *I am going to die!* she realized. She would never finish the afghan now. If she had not been so careless, if she had just concentrated a bit more, if she had not dropped that damned stitch, she *would have* finished. By now the afghan would have been neatly folded in its cardboard storage box, stacked in the closet – all ready to give to … *To whom?* Neville didn't want it – that's what he had said. And just at that instant, she knew for certain that neither would Dean. Cora burst into tears and started trembling. This was it! She was going to die.

"Lady…Lady," said the man gently. "Look, I'm not gonna hurt you, okay? Just do what I say and I won't hurt you. I promise." He lowered the tire iron to his side and squinted down at Cora, gauging the impact of his words – the same way Dr. Braverman had done when he told her about the cancer. Cora wiped her eyes with the sleeve of her sweater, still sobbing, and shaking her head back and forth from side to side. "Where's your purse?" he said softly.

"It – It's in the kitchen. There. On the table." She pointed past him to the cracked leather change purse lying in the middle of the kitchen table next to a half-eaten box of Matzo crackers, a small stack of neatly trimmed coupons, and a form letter from the chemistry chairman soliciting donations from the university's friends and alumni to ensure the continued great success of Gerhard's former colleagues. The man stepped backward toward the kitchen, keeping his eyes on Cora as he moved but stealing backward glances at the change purse. His red canvas high tops made a moist squish each time he pressed down his heels. Once in the kitchen, he slid the tire iron under his arm and snapped open the little purse, digging inside it with his fingers. He pulled out three crisp bills and unfolded them.

"This is it?" he called to her. "Twenty-six bucks? This is all you got?"

"Yes," Cora said. "And the change. There's at least two or three dollars in change."

He refolded the bills, stuffed them into his back pocket, then dumped the change into his palm. He stared at the coins, swirled them in his hand, then dropped them, jingling, into his shirt pocket. "All right," he said. "What do you say we make this easy? You help me out and I'll get out of here a whole lot sooner. Deal?"

Cora had stopped crying now, but her temples throbbed wildly. "What else do you want?" she said.

He pinched thoughtfully at the skin under his chin, glancing around the kitchen – down at the chipped tiled counter, up to the walnut-colored cabinets – then off toward the darkened rooms to his left. "Well, what else you got?" he said at last. "How about silverware. You got some nice silverware?"

"There's some in the drawer next to the sink," she said. "No, the other one, to the left… that's it."

The drawer rolled open with a rusty screech. He reached inside and pulled out a tarnished dinner fork, holding it up to the sink window and twirling it around in the glow of the streetlamp. "Nah," he said, then tossed the fork back into the drawer, closing it with his hip.

Cora did not understand. *Was he stupid?* Maybe it wasn't the finest silver in the world, but it was certainly valuable. Gerhard had purchased the set in Vienna nearly thirty years ago, and he had paid close to a hundred dollars then. Still, she sighed with relief when he closed the drawer.

"What else?" he said.

"The TV?" Cora asked.

He spun around and pointed at the beige, thirteen-inch television set resting on the counter next to the sink. "*This* one?"

"That's it," she said.

He pulled the plastic knob of the set and several seconds later, a Matlock rerun flickered into focus. "Black and white," he said, chuckling, "Unbelievable." He snapped the set off. "What about…jewelry? You have some nice jewelry?"

"Not really," Cora stammered. *What else does he want from me?* "It's in the bedroom, what I have."

"Show me," he said.

Cora raised herself up from the chair, carefully, hoping her quivering legs would support her.

"Lady," he said suddenly, "I have to use the toilet. Down here?" He pointed down the darkened hall to his left with the tire iron.

She nodded.

"Okay, come with me." He started to move quickly down the corridor, then stopped. "Just come where I can see you, I mean. Stand so I can see you through the door."

Cora followed him down the darkened hall and stopped at the door on the right. "It's here," she said. He had walked past the bathroom and into the bedroom at the end of the hall but stopped now, and walked back to her.

"Okay, you stand here and don't move."

He's just a boy, she thought. Up close, she could see that his face was flecked with patches of scraggly yellow hair – so thin and patchy that she had not even noticed them until now. *How desperately this boy was trying to grow a man's beard.* And so, he had let these few hairs grow for weeks – maybe even months – hoping in time they would knit themselves into a beard.

"Just stand there," he said, holding the tire iron under his arm and fumbling with the zipper of his corduroys. He had kept the door open but had not turned on the light, so she saw him in silhouette only. She listened to the stream of urine surge into the water for over a minute, and then the spatter of droplets onto the plastic seat cover as he shook himself. In spite of herself, Cora smiled and shook her head, reminded of Gerhard, who never raised the seat either and never bothered to wipe it down after he finished.

"Okay," he said, zipping up his pants. He walked into the hallway, paused, and then returned to the bathroom, groping one side of the toilet for a handle and then the other before he found it and flushed. He walked back into the hall. "All right, let me see the jewelry."

Cora followed him into the bedroom and pointed toward the squat, mahogany dresser across from the bed. "In the top drawer," she said. "There's a little box."

"Turn on the light," he said. "No, wait. Never mind." He switched on a small lamp on top of the dresser and knelt down onto the worn hardwood floor. The light from the tiny bulb filtered through the emerald shade and cast sickly green shadows against his pale face. "Top drawer?"

Cora nodded.

He slid the heavy drawer open halfway and peered inside, poking Cora's slips and bras to the side with his tire iron. "This it?" He held up a small, hinged box, carved with rose blossoms and a lacy, circular pattern.

She nodded.

He placed the box on the dresser, slid the lamp closer, and opened the lid. Cora watched him sift through the contents with his fingers. "Not much for jewelry are you?" he said. "Wait, this is nice." He held up Gerhard's gold pocket watch and dangled it back and forth before his eyes like a hypnotist. He turned it over and read the inscription: *For my dear husband, Gerhard, with all my love.*

"Husband?" he asked suspiciously, his eyes narrowing as he said the word. "I thought you said you lived here alone."

"I do," she said quickly. "I swear. My husband is dead. I wouldn't lie to you."

"Good." He turned the watch over in his hands for a few seconds. "So you'd rather I didn't take this?"

Cora felt dizzy with relief. "Yes, please."

He tugged at the wisps of hair on his chin, thinking, then slipped the watch into his front pants pocket, stuffing in the fob after it. "I have to, Lady," he said apologetically. "There's nothing else here and I gotta have *something*."

"I understand," she said. *If he would just leave!*

From the sitting room they heard the cuckoo's muffled trill, announcing the quarter hour. Cora chuckled once…then again…then burst out in uncontrolled laughter. She tried to stop but the effort only made her laugh harder. The man stared blankly at her, confused at first, and then he started chuckling too. "What's so funny?" he said.

Cora shook her head, gasping for breath, and reached down to clutch her stomach, laughing hysterically. "My…husband…could not really speak the best English. He was Austrian!" She howled with laughter after this pronouncement and reached for the dresser to steady herself. The man watched her, confused, and began chuckling harder himself. Cora continued. "He…he…didn't always use the right word, like the word for 'weights' – those weights on a cuckoo clock that you have to wind at night –"

"Yeah…"

"And so one night… he got up suddenly from the bed…right after he got in…and I said to him, 'where are you going?' and he said…"

"What did he say?"

"And he said, he said, 'I…I…forgot to put up my balls!'" The man grabbed his sides and roared with laughter. "He…he meant he forgot to wind the clock," Cora explained. Then her laughter stopped abruptly and she began to cry. "Please, please leave. What else do you want from me?"

The man stopped laughing and stared at her with a wounded look. "Lady, I said I wouldn't hurt you. I told you that, remember? I was just going to leave now, anyway. Lady?" Cora had covered her eyes with the palms of her hands and was shaking her head from side to side but did not answer. He chewed his lip, watched her for several seconds, then fished the watch out of his tight pants pocket and set it atop the dresser. "Look, I won't take this," he said. "How's that?"

Cora peeked through her fingers. He pointed at the watch. "Thank you," she whispered. He glanced around the room one last time, then walked past her into the hallway – past the bathroom, through the kitchen, and turned into the sitting room. Cora wiped her eyes with her sleeve, took a deep breath, and after a few moments followed him.

He was kneeling near the door, slipping the tire iron into his cavernous knapsack. He turned his head as she entered. "What's in here?" he said, reaching over to knock on the closet door.

"Just a closet," she said.

He stood up, smoothed his corduroys and opened it. "Hey! Now look at all this. And to think I almost missed it." He swatted the darkness overhead for the string to turn on the bulb, found it, and pulled. "What do you have in these?" He hoisted a box from one of the stacks and set it on the floor, then slipped off the cover and peered down at an azure blue baby blanket. He lifted a corner of the blanket, groped the bottom of the box underneath it, then smoothed it back down. "Are these all blankets?"

"Mostly. There's some sweaters, too. And scarves. Oh, and some woolen caps for winter."

He took down another box from the stack and set it alongside the first, lifted off the cover and knelt down to examine the purple and white afghan she had considered offering Dean. He rubbed the blanket with the backs of his fingers. "Did you make this?"

"I made all of them," she said. "Everything in that closet, I made."

He nodded and stroked the fabric. "Real nice. Beautiful actually. You sell these or something?"

"No, I make them for my family."

"You must have some big family." He stood up. "Okay, Lady, now listen: I've been real nice to you because you didn't give me any trouble. And I'm leaving now. But do *not* call the cops, you understand?"

"I won't. I swear I won't."

"Good. I believe you." He slung the knapsack over his shoulder and nodded down at the floor. "These really are beautiful," he said, tapping against a box with his toe, "Okay, then...."

"Why don't you take one?" she blurted out. *Why not?* Neville never wanted one. Dean never wanted one. They already had one of her blankets – that's what they always said – God forbid they should take two. *Besides, what will I do with them?*

"Are you sure?" he said.

Cora nodded.

"Are you positive?"

"Yes."

"Well, okay then, maybe I will."

"Take any one you want," she said.

He knelt down and scooped up the purple and white afghan from its box. "This one." He studied it closely as it lay cradled in his arms, then knelt down to begin stuffing it inside his knapsack.

"Will it fit?" she said. "I can get you a garbage bag to put it in..."

"No, it'll fit." He pushed and pressed, flattened it down with his hands, then slowly dragged the zipper closed, careful not to snag the yarn. "You know, maybe this wasn't such a waste after all. Thanks, Lady." He opened the door and stepped into the hallway. "You'll have to get this fixed," he said, snapping off a sliver of wood from the splintered doorjamb. "I'm sorry about that." He turned and began to descend the flight of wooden steps. Cora closed the door, pressed into it with her shoulder, and slid the deadbolt into place.

It's over, she thought. *Thank God!* She switched on the lights, staggered over to Gerhard's favorite chair, and slumped down onto the cushion. Cora slipped off her soft, padded slippers and lifted her feet onto the stool. She was chilled and trembling and her teeth were chattering uncontrollably. She reached down for the afghan she had been working on and flipped it up onto her legs, spreading it out, smoothing it, covering herself right up to her chin. Later, after she had rested, she would have to wipe down the toilet seat and put those boxes back in the closet.

She considered calling Neville or Dean, but why frighten them? The man had not hurt her, he had not taken very much – what, twenty-six dollars? Neville and Dean, they had worries of their own now – the last thing they needed was to worry about her, too. *He really liked that afghan,* she thought with a smile. *He could have taken anything from me but all he wanted was one of my afghans.*

She looked down at the zigzags of the afghan covering her. Another six rows and it would be finished – sometime tomorrow, or maybe Wednesday. *What's the rush? When I finish, I finish.* Neville had been right about one thing. There were no deadlines to meet.

Photo: Sergey Gorshkov

*Ed Bachrach is the retired Chairman and CEO of Bachrach Clothing, Inc.,
a national retailer of men's fashions. He is producing a feature film about
Frank Lloyd Wright from a screenplay that he has written. He resides in
Chicago and Decatur, Illinois.*

Geese

By Ed Bachrach

I

THE FIRM, STRONG FEMALE GOOSE flew in the third position of the V formation as she headed north in the predawn darkness. She and the others, all thirteen of them, had been flying since the sun rose the previous day. As they flew in and out of the clouds in the dark, moonless night, they honked continuously, signaling to each other things that were unnecessary when they were on the ground. Those who had flown the route before signaled the direction they sensed they should fly. The young ones, whose first trip it was, honked to check their position in order to keep in the tail draft of the lead gander.

It was early in the spring of an unusually harsh winter. Having fattened in the warm wintering grounds next to the winding river that flowed into the big sea, they were ready to come north for the summer and to have their young ones again. When it was time to go, the lead male flew high in the air several times a day for three days, until he sensed that the wind from the south would give them a good carry. Coming back to the others on the ground, he called them to the sky for this first leg of the trip. Now they had flown so many hours that their energy was spent, and it was time to rest, eat, and regain strength.

When they flew, they found their way with senses that they couldn't understand. If the sun or moon or stars were out, it seemed natural that these objects would be where they were supposed to be at any time. If they got off course, it just didn't feel right and they adjusted. Now they had been in the clouds for several hours and that same sense came to them. The clouds were getting lighter in color as the sun came around the other side of the land below them. Just as the sun began to shine, they broke through the clouds and found themselves following the shore of the big lake: just where they knew they would be.

The lead gander scoured the ground for a safe resting place and sighted a marsh where two branches of a stream joined each other, flowing into the big lake. He let out a double honk and started his descent to the stream as it met the lake. The others followed him down to the water. They rested in the water for a few moments, then waddled to shore and began eating the fresh sprouts of grass.

The thirteen geese consisted of the big gander, two smaller ganders, the strong female and another smaller female, and eight goslings that had grown to be almost the size of adults. It was their first trip, but they already knew the way of feeding. The group would send out sentinels in three or four directions while the rest ate in peace. The guards would eat if they could, but they had to keep their heads up and their ears tuned to danger. After awhile they would shift and send others to guard. There was much eating to do in the next two or three days, before they would fly again.

ON THE GROUND MANY PACES TO THE WEST, a man stepped out of his teepee at sunrise and watched the geese as they flew lower and lower. His spirits rose. It was a frosty morning, so he stepped back into the teepee to put more wood on the fire while his wife and little girl slept. This was one of three teepees in a small clan of people who had roamed this area for many, many years. Just days ago he had moved with this clan of eleven from the ridge further west.

He and his clan had just been through a hard winter. There was much snow and coldness, and the game was hard to find and difficult to kill. The little meat and nuts that had been gathered the last summer were long gone, and his flesh clung to his bones. Any food he could find he gave to his wife so she would not dry up and starve the toddler. But now the snow was gone, and he was hunting, trapping, and fishing again. Outside the teepee he had built a small rack to dry the meats in the rising sun.

He was not the only creature to notice the geese. Many paces south of the camp, a solitary coyote walked along an old deer trail and was just under a tree when he heard the honking. Loping out from under a branch, he looked up in the early light to see the geese fly to the big lake. He, too, was heartened. It had been a winter filled with hardship and hunger. Now seeing the first geese of the season, his ears perked up and he started off on the roundabout way through trails across the stream, jumping the long tufts of dead grass on his way to the big lake.

It was a long time later that the coyote was close enough to slow his pace and begin to quietly stalk toward the sound of the geese. The wind was from the south and the geese could smell danger. The large gander was nearest to the coyote, and when he spotted the animal he let out a series of honks. Instantly the birds were airborne. The discouraged coyote backed away to the cover of a bush and lay waiting for the geese to return. After a while, he smelled smoke from the new camp and headed off in that direction.

At the teepee the man and woman had taken a few strips of meat from inside and laid them on the wooden rack for drying. The man gave the woman a large strip and told her to eat it. He ate a small one, just enough to give him energy to make it through the day. When he was finished, he picked up a flint knife and a smaller scraper and headed east toward where the geese had landed.

The man walked north along the creek bank to a clump of willow trees. The sun was getting higher in the sky, and the wind from the south felt good on his back. Stopping at the trees, the man took the large flint knife and started cutting large strips of bark from the side of the small willow shoots. There were no leaves on the trees, but inside the bark the familiar green told the man that the warm, leafy days were coming. After cutting a few strips, he used the smaller scraper to form thin, sturdy strips of bark. He tied three small strips to the trunk of one of the small trees and braided them into a long rope that was very strong. Finishing that one, he made four more.

With these five ropes he walked east to the shore of the lake and looked at the small game and deer trails that led from the water inland. He was looking for places where he could tie one end of a rope to a tree and form a loop with the other. These snares had always worked to catch the animals and birds as they sped along the trail. He found three good sites but couldn't find suitable anchors for the other two. By now it was late in the afternoon, and he took the two remaining ropes as he headed back to the teepee.

SHORTLY AFTER HE HAD LEFT THE TEEPEE THAT MORNING, the woman left their toddler with a woman who lived in another teepee that was a few feet from theirs and walked to the stream to fill a leather pouch with water. The other woman was busy, and the little girl wandered out of the teepee. Not long after she left, the coyote came near the camp. Coming around a gray, leafless bush, he spotted the few strips of meat on the wooden rack outside the teepee. He stopped in his tracks and listened intently, then sniffed the air to see if danger was near. Then he lowered his stance near the ground and started slowly stalking toward the teepee.

He had just moved forward when, to his surprise, the little girl toddled into his view. She was wearing a cover of animal skin that barely covered her behind. There was crusted waste from her behind running down her leg to her bare feet, and he could now smell it. He paused for a moment but then resumed creeping forward until he was within 20 paces of the teepee. He stopped again, and his gaze went from the meat to the little child. He couldn't reason but seemed to be waiting for some impulse inside to tell him whether to snatch the meat or try for the little girl. In an instant he heard something to his side, but before he could discern what it was, a large stone grazed his hindquarters. Turning in the direction of the sound he saw the woman and she followed the stone throw with a shrill sound as she charged toward him. Still hungry, he ran away from her and the teepee and headed in to where the geese had been to hunt for smaller game.

In the late afternoon the man returned to the teepee. He had speared two small fish and scraped off the meat from their bodies on a flat stone in the camp. He gave it to the woman to eat, and she told him about the coyote. He stayed in the camp until it was dark and then walked quietly halfway back to where he had set the snares.

When the geese fled the coyote that morning, they flew south of the stream that led into the big lake. The grass there was tall and it was hard to see danger until it was too close to flee. So as the sun got lower in the sky, the big gander waddled up to the strong female, honked, and took flight. The rest followed him as he made his way back to the area they had been in that the morning. Once again, they landed in the water and waddled ashore. The two females and one of the goslings flew west a little ways and took their positions as sentinels.

In the darkening gray just after sunset, the rest of the geese meandered along the slope near the big lake, eating as much grass as they could take in. One female gosling found a stretch that had been beaten down by the feet of deer and rabbits and muskrats that led from the sand of the lake into the grasses. She slowly made her way along this path, plucking the grasses and weeds on either side as she went. As she passed a stunted tree next to the path, she ducked her head to avoid a low-hanging branch that was in her way. Moving forward, she felt the branch move with her. To clear this obstacle she pulled her head up and waddled briskly forward, but as she did she felt the branch close in around her neck. The harder she tried to get away from the branch, the more it grabbed her neck. She thrashed back and forth and side to side but couldn't free herself. Failing at this, she tried to take flight, but the branch pulled her back to the ground where the flapping of her wings could now be heard by others. She let out a muted honk.

The strong female heard the sounds and headed toward them. As she neared, the honks became louder and more urgent. The man who was many paces away heard this and began quietly moving in that direction. From a point that was closer, the coyote took off at a swift lope toward the sound of struggle. He got there first and found the entangled gosling backing away from where the branch was tied to the tree, trying to pull free. Suddenly there appeared in his path the strong female, who faced him, puffed up her feathers, and began honking furiously. His instinct caused him to stop and beware, but something from a different place in him told him that this animal could be food, too. So he charged the strong female as she hissed and fluttered her wings. Now within contact range, he lunged at her, but she had raised herself from the ground and landed a strong peck from her bill on the top of his head. Turning upwards, he nipped at her but missed. She was out of his way now and he could see the trapped gosling a few paces ahead. He ran to the immobile bird while the female fluttered and honked and pecked at him from behind. There was time to look and think because this bird was not going anywhere and was not even moving. The coyote decided to bite the neck of the bird just below the branch. Doing so, he pulled hard but could not free the prey.

While he struggled with the bird, the strong female gave up the fight as the rest of the geese were already in the sky and heading out of sight. She took to the sky honking plaintively. The coyote took his mouth off the neck and looked at the goose in flight. Turning back to the prey he looked around for a moment and heard something coming along the nearby path. He had to act fast. He bit the neck again, harder this time, and pulled it back and forth vigorously. The more he did this the more he could feel the neck coming apart in his mouth. With one hard pull the neck had separated from the body. He opened his mouth and looked around. To his left he could see the man now walking toward him on the path. The man proceeded carefully and held a spear in front of him that had a piece of sharp stone on its tip.

Without thinking, the coyote grabbed the full body of the goose in his jaws and ran toward the lakeshore. The man ran after him but was not as fast. Once on the shore, the coyote ran north for a little way and then, finding another trail, disappeared into the grass. The man lowered his head and began slowly walking back to the teepee.

II

ON A BALMY SPRING EVENING JUST BEFORE THE SUN SET, a string of cars was stopped on the thoroughfare, while a gaggle of geese gingerly waddled across the road. If they could have made sense of the symbols around them, they would have read the two green street signs with white lettering, one saying Halsted and the other Division. Likewise, they would have been able to read the newspaper that blew past them in the gentle wind that had the numbers 1988 on the top.

But they couldn't know this. Years ago they would have flown across the street. Years before that they would have flown over this whole city, because they would have seen danger everywhere. But over the past several years they had stopped those laborious migrations, as there was safety and food aplenty right here in this place. They had even stopped flying so much, because the inhabitants of this land let them waddle where and when they pleased. Now they had been feeding on the new shoots of grass that were emerging from the shores of the river just to the west. This river was quiet and peaceful, and the only danger was the trash, the plastic bags, and the bottles that floated by or had become entangled in the branches on the shore.

It had been a mild winter, and the people living nearby in the towers called Cabrini Green were out and about enjoying the warm gusty breeze from the south. This clump of high-rise buildings nestled into the land just east of the north branch of the river and north of Division Street had stood for about as long as the geese had stopped migrating. They had been built by this grand city for those whom fortune had failed to favor.

By the time the sun set, the geese had arrived in a muddy yard with little new grass bordered by Division and Larrabee streets. One of the tall buildings rose near this muddy field. The building was faced with horizontal courses of gray, dirty brick that were broken every eight feet up either by a wide window or a heavy steel screen that covered a balcony.

The only way any thing or person could come and go from the building was through a single entrance on the ground floor in the middle of the building. The entrance rested on a raised platform with a rusted broken guard rail on the side and crumbling steps down to a cracked sidewalk that led to the street.

Under the platform and adjoining the foundation of the building lived a colony of rats. They were just a few of the millions of rats that had inhabited the city since its founding. They could eat practically any refuse the city could offer up, and the labyrinth of structures and sewers created more natural homes than the men in the city had built. The rats multiplied so prolifically that the population was resilient to disaster, even if the individual rats were vulnerable. This evening, the adult rats darted furtively around the building, unnoticed by the humans and geese nearby.

High up the building on the fourteenth floor, the sound of voices could be heard from a room just inside a door that opened into one of the prisonlike balconies. There were two men, a younger woman, and a two-year-old little girl. The apartment was the home of Yolanda and her daughter Leticia. Yolanda was plump but well-groomed in her acid-washed jeans, white sneakers, and purple V-neck ribbed sweater. Unlike her mother, Leticia was thin, with her delicate hair braided into two long pigtails. Between those two pigtails lay a face of innocence full of giggles, squeals of laughter, and curiosity.

Yolanda's boyfriend Donnie had lived on and off with her for eighteen months but was not Leticia's father. He was tall and lanky in his baggy jeans and white sweatshirt with a designer logo on the chest. His hair was long, forming a curly, fuzzy hemisphere around his thin, flat face. His buddy Anton had stopped by to sell him a nickel bag of marijuana and smoke a joint with him. Anton was a stocky, shorter man with a sunny disposition.

Donnie's disposition had been rather foul this day. He had quarreled with Yolanda the previous night, and she had made him sleep on the sofa in the living room that was too short for his large frame. The fight had kept him up late, and Leticia was up early disrupting his sleep. He had never really worked and didn't have any money of his own, so asking Yolanda for money this morning was awkward. He was not from this neighborhood and had to beware of the gangs that controlled these buildings. He carried a semiautomatic pistol with nine rounds in the magazine for protection in his large front pocket.

He had a Cherry Coke and a corn dog for lunch and started drinking Colt 45s around three in the afternoon. Now with Anton here, he saw his first friendly face of the day. Yolanda and Leticia had gone to the corner store, and the two men rolled a couple of large joints and finished the first one in ten minutes, during which they said little. Donnie threw the roach in the toilet and got two 45s out of the refrigerator, opened them, and gave one to Anton. They were halfway through their beers when Yolanda and Leticia walked in.

"What you been doin' in here," Yolanda said, glaring at Donnie. "Smell like weed."

"I ain't done nuthin'. Just hangin' wit' Anton," Donnie replied.

Yolanda put two plastic bags of groceries on the counter and started emptying them. When Donnie spotted an extra-large bag of Ruffles potato chips, he got up and grabbed them from the counter. Yolanda gave him a cold stare but didn't say a thing. Donnie had become so selfish and inconsiderate lately, but she still remembered how sweet and loving he was when they first met. She could sense her feelings for him turning sour, but she still enjoyed his loving so much when they were getting along. And she knew that if she lost him, it would not be easy finding and holding onto another man. She hadn't seen Leticia's father since before Leticia was born.

When she had finished putting the food away, she sent Leticia to the bedroom and went to the hall bathroom. She had only poked her head in when she came storming back into the living room.

"Why you lie to me, Donnie? What that roach in the stool?" she said angrily, but in a hushed voice so that Leticia wouldn't hear.

Just then Leticia came out of the bedroom and the conversation stopped. The child wandered up to the men, and then she spotted the Ruffles on the table. She grabbed the bag of chips and headed for the bedroom. Donnie could not hide the anger in his eyes as he rose, chased her down, and grabbed the bag away from her. Two chips fell out of the bag, and Leticia began to cry. Yolanda picked up the little girl and turned to Donnie as he retreated to the sofa.

"You two get yo' asses outta here. You nothin' but trouble," she yelled.

"C'mon, let's go downstairs," Donnie said to Anton.

Donnie threw Yolanda a defiant glare but didn't put up a fight. He picked up the remaining joint, the Ruffles, and his 45. The two men walked out the door to the apartment and down the grim hallway to the elevator, which was scratched and decorated with graffiti.

In the muddy field the geese pecked at what grass they could find, but they mostly nested in the security of the yard. Between them and the building, a rat smelled a small firm cylinder of goose dropping, then ran elsewhere in search of something more suitable to eat. With the exception of traffic on Division Street, the night was quiet when the geese saw the two men come out of the building in the dim light of the solitary light bulb overhead.

"I goin' on. This ain't my hood," said Anton, and he took off down the cracked sidewalk with the gaggle of geese nesting on either side.

"Thanks, man," Donnie replied as he found a seat on the platform and put the bag of Ruffles between his feet on the step below him.

He had had just two sips of beer when Yolanda and Leticia came out.

"You just a pig. We want nothin' to do wit' you." Yolanda had the last word as she took her little girl out for a walk to cool off.

Donnie could say nothing, so he watched the two walk the same cracked walk. Leticia started chasing after the geese, but Yolanda pulled her arm back and hurried her pace. Donnie took a big swig of the beer and shook his head. He was mad at Yolanda, mad at himself, and mad at this fucked-up life of his. Exasperated, he put down his beer. The gun in his pocket was digging into his hip, so he pulled it out and set it on the platform next to him. He reached in his pocket and pulled out the joint and a cigarette lighter. He lit the joint, took a starter drag, and put the lighter back in his pocket. As the marijuana seeped into his head, he could feel the worries fade away, and he looked up at the lazy sliver of moon that had just cleared the next building. Now life was better.

After a moment he put the joint to his lips and took another long drag, holding it in for what seemed like a minute. This time the sensation in his head was more intense and, although not unpleasant, it made him want to lie back and relax. As he slowly reclined on the concrete platform his foot kicked the bag of Ruffles and they spilled down the steps.

The geese spotted the chips and started waddling from each side of the sidewalk and onto the walk itself, hurrying toward the food. They were high-stepping now, and all were honking excitedly. Hearing this, Donnie arose and looked down the sidewalk in a haze. His excited and altered consciousness could only sense the amplified honking and the movement of this brown mass toward him, and he was afraid. He picked up his gun and pointed it at the mass. He pulled the trigger and heard the sharp crack of detonation. The mass in front of him started to rise as the geese took flight. He fired again, down the walkway this time where they had been, but not where they were. He fired three more times into the flock as it rose in the air. Then he stopped and could smell the salty aroma of the gun smoke as it wafted toward him. It was silent now, but just for a moment.

From the sidewalk came a loud shriek of pain.

"Aiyhhh! My baby!" Yolanda wailed as she knelt by the limp body of Leticia and the pool of blood nearby.

Donnie sat on the step in a stupor and looked toward the spot where Yolanda was kneeling. He was paralyzed by inaction. As he stared ahead, a rat approached the fallen chips and took one in its mouth, then disappeared around the corner of the building.

In the spring darkness the geese made a brief low flight back to the river and began nibbling on the spring grass.

Mary Erhard grew up in Chicago and is a writer and editor. She enjoys reading, running and traveling with her husband and four children.

West Side Story

By Mary Erhard

WOLF SAW THE MAN pass the money to Jimmy.

He was there all of a sudden out of nowhere, a youngish man in a loose yellow shirt that drifted over a small paunch and clung to his jeans, clean and stiff and bright blue with newness. He was talking to Jimmy, the two of them standing together near the door. But Wolf spotted the passing of the bill down low, the man finding Jimmy's hand and slipping it to him quick and quiet while with his other hand he fanned a wad of stapled folded pages in front of Jimmy's face. The bill looked like a $50, but it might have been more.

It was no accident that Wolf clocked the transaction. He scanned the residence's common areas constantly as he moved the wide push-broom across the beige-flecked tile, down the two hallways where the men's bedrooms were, and around the open foyer, keeping an eye out for trouble. No, he didn't have to sweep; the men at the Crossroads Sober Living House had no official chores, other than to get themselves off the dole and into jobs, meanwhile gathering strength as they transitioned from being practicing to recovering alcoholics, supposedly. But he liked to keep busy, and he liked things to be as neat as they could. He moved a little closer, sweeping.

"I'll give you another one of those if you fill it out and send it to me," the man told Jimmy.

There was a mistake. He shouldn't give Jimmy any money. Jimmy would take the $50 and immediately deposit it at his favorite spending institution, the bank of the ABC Discount Wine and Spirits Package Liquor Store a half a block away, if he got the chance. It was all Wolf could do to keep him on the (relatively) straight and narrow, and that was only really working because Jimmy's current status was broke. That cash, that cash would go the way of Krapp's last tape.

What could this man want with Jimmy? ... who was looking at the man and trying to hold his eyes straight, like he did when he wanted it to look like he was paying attention. The man said something Wolf couldn't catch, and Wolf moved closer, behind the rack of used clothes from the Sally Ann's, so the man wouldn't see him.

"It's easy ... [more words Wolf couldn't hear. It was like listening to a badly tuned radio] ... and I'll give you another $50."

"Oh yeah, sure." Jimmy could sound so reasonable.

"So you'll do it, right? Fill it out and send it to me." He handed Jim a big white envelope.

A bad feeling was settling into Wolf's bones, but he didn't let it distract him.

"Right," Jimmy said.

"All of it, right?"

"Right."

The man turned to go, giving Wolf the once-over as he passed the rack on the way to the door, and Jaybert, who had been watching the interaction by the wall, made for the stranger once the connection had broken between him and Jimmy.

"'Scuse me. 'Scuse me, do you know of any jobs?" But Jaybert was soft-spoken and anyway the man was long gone, through the door fast – hadn't even heard or let on if he had. He had gone, leaving behind an unsettled feeling that showed in Jaybert's face and in the way Jimmy scuttled down the hall toward his bedroom, white folded papers sticking out of his baggy back pocket. But Wolf was quick, and he sidled into the room right behind him. Jimmy sat on the bed and lit a smoke.

"So what's going on? Jim? You made a little money, I see. What's with those papers?" Wolf asked.

"Nothing."

"C'mon, what'd he tell you?"

"Oh, uh, he said the Reverend Clarence recommended me." Now casually proud, as though this were the most reasonable thing in the world. Jimmy's moods changed fast as clouds across a March sky. "He told him to look for me. Said I'd be a good person to answer a questionnaire."

"What kind of questionnaire? What does he want to know?"

"Oh. Uh, let's see." He pulled the pages from his back pocket and pawed them open. "Oh yeah. Yeah." He scanned the top page, then looked at Wolf. "It's easy stuff." He rubbed at the bottom to turn the page, but it kept slipping from his grasp.

"Jim, you're like a bear cub with gloves on. Let's have a look-see."

Jimmy handed him the pages, and Wolf looked at them carefully. Jimmy stood up and looked over his shoulder.

"It's just stuff about me. Right?" Sure and unsure, one second to the next.

Wolf looked up. "He paid you? He give you money?" There were three white pages, but not dense – they were filled with prompts in big type: name, address, social security number, each followed by one or several lines for the answers.

"Uh, yeah, yeah." Enthused now, eyes wide and excited, he moved closer to Wolf. "Fifty bucks," he said on the sly. "I mean, what the fuck. Just for, like, answering questions."

"Did he tell you why he wants it?"

"What?"

"Why does he want all this information about you?"

Even though the spaces were big, this man whoever would wind up with a lot of data on Jimmy. There was room for financial information, too: social security number, card numbers, account numbers. In fact, it looked like a credit card or bank account application, although there was no institution's name on the form.

"He's an idiot. I mean, come on. Why does he want to know about me? I mean, he's not the draft board! 'We want you!' Those morons. Fucking military fucking political morons."

Jimmy was heading toward his anti-government jag.

"Look here, what about this? What are you going to say about this? This one." Wolf showed him the question: 'Have you ever been convicted of a felony?' "You were inside. For dealing. Remember?"

"He doesn't have to know that. Fuck that. The fuck does he care? It's none of his goddam business." Jimmy grabbed the pages and stuffed them into his back pocket. "What can he do to me? And look. He said he's gonna send me another fifty bucks when I send this back. Just for filling it out. Aaaah. He won't know I been inside. He'll never know."
Jimmy got up abruptly and made for the door.

"Where you going, Jim?"

"What?" Dreamy innocence, like he'd forgotten, but Wolf knew where he was headed.

"Maybe you should fill this out first, before you go out. Want some help with that?"

"Naw, I'll do it later."

"Best now. Here."

Wolf reached for the sheets, irritating Jimmy sufficiently that he didn't notice Wolf slip the $50 from out of his shirt pocket and palm it. Jimmy grabbed the sheets back, then lay down for a nap, curling protectively around them.

Wolf wondered, what was this man doing here? Why did the Reverend Clarence allow him to make the offer? The other men would be angry when they knew Jimmy had been favored.

But even more than that, who was he? An undercover cop? Would Jimmy be arrested? Was he trying to catch Jimmy at something he'd done, or didn't do? And he was taking advantage of Jimmy, that was for sure, and that meant sometime, whether in ten days or ten years, Jim would suffer from this encounter, even if only with a night in jail.

Of course, Jimmy didn't see that. He didn't think ahead. Or when he did, it was to the cash in hand and the prospect of more, and what it would buy that he currently couldn't pay for.

Wolf would find this man again. The big envelope lay partially crushed and unnoticed under the sleeping Jimmy, but the upper-left corner was visible and showed only a name that Wolf assumed was false: John Fair. Too simple, but some names were.

But once outside the building, this John Fair had made a call from his cell phone that Wolf had observed. He had stood on the windy corner and punched in a number before crossing the street to a sport utility vehicle and getting in and driving away. Wolf had excellent eyesight, and had seen the white words pop up on the blue screen before they disappeared under the man's square-tipped finger when he punched the selection: "Promised Land Su..."

It was a simple matter to go around the corner to the public library and look this name up: Promised Land Supportive Living Center, at an address on the north side. He could go there and look around, see who Fair might have contacted. Anyone who would be called by this character would stand out clear as day to Wolf. But he probably wouldn't have to go anywhere. The questionnaire would probably wind up in a crumple under Jimmy's bed.

Later, Wolf made a show of suggesting they go out for a bite with that fifty dollars, and Jaybert and Edgar saw that Jimmy had lost it already. About two a.m. a fight broke out between Edgar and the new man in room C. The Rev. Clarence got up and yelled at them before Edgar had the time to do more than cut his arm, although the new man moaned all night down the halls.

Wolf put the events in the back of his mind until a few days later, when he saw Jimmy shifting from foot to foot by the front door, looking out the glass and fingering a large white envelope, then ducking out and across the street and back lickety-split on bouncy feet, hands empty and mind clear.

Wolf tidied his room – if that was possible, as it was already tight as Jimmy's grip on a half-pint – then stood in the doorway of the office, where Rev. Clarence was picking up file folders from the floor. He turned his head sidelong and saw Wolf.

"Come in, come on in, Wolf," he said, straightening up, which wasn't a long trip since Rev. Clarence was short and squat. The black shirt under the white collar was wrinkled, and the collar itself had dark streaks.

He set the folders down, put on his welcoming-the-flock face, then sat down, waiting a beat for Wolf to speak before making an elaborate gesture toward the opposite chair. His face had a fine sheen of perspiration.

"What can I do for you this fine morning?"

Wolf stayed by the door. "I'll be away for a couple-three days, maybe a week," he said.

"Away? Now, now you know that's not possible, Wolf." Stuttering a little, like he did when one of the men contradicted him. "Here is where you live and here is where you stay. Out there you are but a stranger in a strange land." A little lilt at that last, in his sing-songy Bible-lecturing voice. Wolf's eyes narrowed and his gut tightened.

"You stay here continuously" – con-tin-u-ous-ly, he said – "until you find a job that supports you. That is our agreement."

"I won't be longer than a week."

The Rev. Clarence wrinkled his nose like he smelled something bad. "You going on a drunk?" he said, and snorted. "Huh. You going on a drinking trip." The reverend dropped his "ares" and "haves" when he was mad. "Going back to the gutter, ain't you. You like it, you miss it. You homesick for the puke and trash. You, you..." He shook his head, breathing heavily, and began fooling with papers on his desk. "You go, you don't come back," he said to the desk. That was a threat. Then he looked up at Wolf with a sneer.

"You nothing but a drunk-ass bum," he said.

Wolf may have drunk too much in the past (in fact, he surely had). He may have lain in the gutter or wherever Rev. Clarence chose to say he had been, made no difference to him, he didn't care. But no one could give him a name and tell him what or who he was or wasn't. Rev. Clarence couldn't call him bum or fool or genius or the second coming of Christ or stranger in a strange land as if those words represented the sum total and outer limits of Wolf. But he let it go.

"Why did you send John Fair to see Jimmy?" Wolf asked.

Rev. Clarence snapped his head back as though Wolf had taken a swing at him, and half-rose from his chair. But on the way up he gave a lightning glance to the top of his desk and pushed the cracked-open top left drawer closed. He looked Wolf in the eye.

"You get outta here," he said.

Wolf rested his raised arm on the door frame and turned to go. "I'll be back," he said. "Don't give my room away."

WOLF WALKED OUT THE DOOR into the damp, overcast day and went around the corner to the bus stop. Forty-five minutes later, he stepped off at the corner of a busy intersection. The air was chill with a fresh breeze from the lake, and Wolf pulled in vain at the sleeves of the too-short jacket he had grabbed from the rack when leaving the Crossroads. Per the bus driver's instruction, he turned into the first side street on the left.

The sounds of traffic receded almost immediately, and the neighborhood was pretty. Tree branches sprouting with tender green leaves made a canopy over the sidewalk. The curbs and the stone and wooden stairs leading to the trim doorways were free of garbage, and the people on the streets were few and clean – a young woman in a colorful scarf pushed a small child in a stroller; a man in a suit walked briskly forward. Wolf felt like a stick man drawn in pencil on this color photo, smudged and flimsy and hard to see.

And just past the turn in the winding block was the thing itself: the Promised Land Supportive Living Center, a tall, rangy building whose outside at least lived up to its name, made of new-looking bright beige brick, and with the notched edges of a deep green awning flapping in the breeze over broad double glass doors.

But all along the front of the building, like mayflies marring the perfection of a summer night, were loose groupings of rough-looking people. They looked like mooches, Wolf thought, but there were more of them than usually gathered in one place.

In fact, if it weren't for the fancy overhang and fresh exterior, he could be looking at the Crossroads Sober Living House. The men – and women – loitering around the front, smoking and talking, alone or in groups, were cut from the same cloth.

Or almost. Not exactly. Actually, when you looked up close, most of these people were not like Jaybert, say, quietly panhandling for jobs. That one with the muscles and the jailhouse tats, for example, asked him for money, then swore at him when told he had none, and had mean eyes too, like he would do worse than cut somebody with a blunt penknife when no one was looking in the night. And there was the stony-faced young black kid whose wheelchair was blocking anybody's path to the big double doors. And the others just milling around with their sizing-up glances. And all of them splayed out against that pretty building.

Wolf passed them all and walked inside, into a large, expansive lobby, with many people milling about. People like himself, down at heel. People from the regular world, in their crisp colorful clothes. People in scrubs.

Scrubs? Now that he had caught sight of them, they seemed to be everywhere. Was this a hospital? A nursing home? But no, the non-nurse's aide people – the inmates, the others – were not old.

And this lobby room was just too nice. The walls were a warm adobe, and the whole room was flooded with light: pouring from the windows, bouncing off shiny surfaces, streaming down from skylights. And also, there was none of the unholy tang of Lysol battling urine.

But though there were a few people from the real world here, again there was that disconnect. Many of the people were marginal: a pale man whose head rested unsupported on his shoulder, rolling a wheelchair up a ramp (there were a great number of ramps). A sloppy fat woman wearing enormous sweats who sat in an electric wheelchair in front of the wide-screen TV. A fellow who looked like Jimmy who loped along the back wall with a swagger. And across the room, sitting at a computer screen, a small woman with thick, brushy hair who appeared to be watching him.

What was this place, and what did it have to do with Jimmy? The Promised Land against all odds appeared to welcome Wolf's fellow travelers. Why? The link so far was John Fair. He would look for Fair, but on the quiet. On the other hand, maybe Jimmy's name would turn over a few rocks.

Wolf surveyed the great room. On the left was a countertop with a clipboard. A girl with nice hair was on the phone; he approached the window hesitantly and addressed her bent head.

"Excuse me. Do you know where I might find Jimmy McCourt?"

She looked up and smiled immediately at him, cradling the phone receiver in her hand. "Who?" she asked.

"Jimmy McCourt. Do you know him?" he asked.

"No, but there are a lot of people I don't know," she said. "I'm sorry, our system is down right now. If you'll sign in" – a nod at the clipboard – "I'll look up his apartment as soon as I'm finished."

Clipboards were bad news; they often kept track of things that were better left unrecorded. When he nodded his thanks, she turned away, and he immediately cut across the TV and ramp areas to the far corner. Part nursing home and part apartment building? He would make a tour of the place. He scanned a bank of metal-faced mailboxes not visible from his previous vantage point – all numbers, no names – then went down a connecting hallway.

There were three doors: a movie theater, an exercise room, and a shabby room that reeked of cigarettes with black tile flooring and Styrofoam coffee supplies. Though small, this room contained four people, sitting on folding chairs lining the walls and smoking, including the exceptionally large man Wolf spotted earlier, whose bulk and simmering irritability made the room seem even smaller. The man gave him a flat glance, then looked away. The others took no notice of him. Wolf saw the big man produce a small bottle, pour a shot of liquid into his cup, and return the bottle to the recesses of his person quick as a wink in spite of his size. He felt an answering surge in his gut but ignored it and closed the door.

Wolf left the hallway and continued on his circuit of the perimeter. When he reached the computer bank, the woman with the brushy hair who had watched him from afar – it was a wiry mix of shoulder-length salt-and-pepper, he noticed – approached him with an open and curious manner.

"Looking for me?" she said. Her very large gray eyes were fixed on his, and she had to tilt her head up to do it.

"I'm looking for a friend, name of Jimmy McCourt. Know him?"

"I'm Lisa."

"Do you know him? Jimmy McCourt?"

"No. Does he live here?" Her voice had a pleasant raspiness that gave it almost a musical quality.

"You can do that? Live here?"

"Sure. I live here."

"How can I get a place here?"

"Well, that depends. How do you feel? Got anything wrong, if I may be so bold?" She wasn't smiling, but the tone of her voice held the smile implicit.

He would have scanned the room while they talked but her eyes seemed to have hold of his.

"We're all sickies here," she said. "Gimps and cripples. Anyone who can't make it on their own can come and live here."

The ugly words bothered him, but the place was beginning to make sense.

"What does that mean?"

"Say something happened to you, and they put you in a nursing home. But it's full of drooling bags and randy old men and it smells like piss. You might try to kill yourself."

He looked at her wrists, but they were covered by her sleeves. He didn't like the way she talked, but her eyes were as gray as the lake on a windy day.

"If you're lucky, they send you here." She had a silly laugh, which she loosed now. "You get an apartment, you got CNAs to give you your meds, you get three squares a day."

"Really. Everybody sick?"

"Or damaged," she said, now with a half-smile lifting the edges of her mouth. "Joey lost his lower half to a shotgun when his homies blew off."

"Lost it?"

"As good as. He can't use it anymore." She raised her eyebrows. "Any of it. Lewis there," she nodded briefly in the direction of the Jimmy look-alike, then returned her gaze to him, "is nuts, the kind where you can't remember anything. He can't leave lest he forget how to get back. Frank is turning into a baby again. Pretty soon the CNAs will have to start dressing him." That must be the limp man who'd wheeled up the ramp behind him.

"So how do all these…"

"…pathetic fuck-ups afford it?" she said.

Wolf winced at the obscenity.

"The state says we lucky duckies deserve the best, so here we are." She paused. "Medicaid. And Social Security. Oh, yeah, the Promised Land also takes cash." The goofy laugh grated on his nerves.

"So it's legit? This place?"

"Oh, yeah. Completely."

He doubted that, but he let it pass.

"So what are you doing here?" he asked.

Now she smiled full-out. "I can't be trusted to behave myself," she said. "I can't be trusted any farther than you can throw me."

The crown of her head came no higher than his chin.

"I could throw you pretty far," he said.

She made no comment on that but said, "No, but you're looking for someone. Here's where you want to look." She moved toward a different hallway and turned, waiting for him to follow.

"The apartments are down here," she said. "There's one seems like it's always being made up for somebody new. C'mon, I'll show you."

"No need. Just tell me where to find it."

"You sure?" she asked. She stood right in front of him as if to block his way, though he wasn't moving.

He gave a brief nod, and said, "Yep."

She gave him an annoyed look and moved aside, then turned toward the hall and said, "Follow it all the way down, then turn left. It's there." Now she was abrupt and fake-indifferent, and she walked immediately away.

He followed her directions and came to a room whose door was ajar. He pushed it open and scanned the inside – the work of a second, as it was a tiny studio, unfurnished, with flat gray-speckled carpeting and a black and white tiled floor visible from the bathroom. There were a microwave and cooktop along the narrow strip of countertop.

It wasn't much, but like everything else here, it was clean and new, and it looked like a palace compared to his place at the Crossroads, where he shared a small room with the cleaning supplies and extra toilet paper.

Wolf looked out the window, where he saw the brick side of the next building, but with enough room in between the two to let the morning sun stream in. So this little apartment was a place where a man could make a good start, get better, and point toward something new without being reminded of where he came from.

The door opened, and the thick-haired woman was standing there.

"See?" she said.

"Nice," he said. He gave the place one more look, then moved past her out the door.

"This way," she said, walking until she reached a door at the end of the hall.

He was still standing by the empty apartment.

"Want to see my room?" She raised her voice a little to be heard, hand on the doorknob.

He looked at her for a moment, a small shadowed figure in the dark at the end of the hall, then said, "Sure," and followed as she disappeared into the room.

IT WAS TIME WOLF LOCATED JOHN FAIR. Wolf found his name in a Promised Land brochure on a coffee table; he was called Marketing Director, and Wolf figured his office would be in the corridor he hadn't explored. None of the residents, as he learned they were called, were in the hall, and he walked at a steady pace as though he belonged.

Sheila Geraghty, the Nursing Director according to her nameplate, was on the phone as he walked past the first door, making gestures that would be invisible to their recipient and using a stern, harassed voice. The door that had Fair's name on it was half-open, and the office was empty.

The coast was clear and he slipped inside, stepping around the desk immediately to the chair side facing the door. The top was clear of papers and the lower left drawer was locked. Its shape showed that it was likely to have hanging files, and the shallow top drawer slid open. A single fifty-dollar bill rested amid the pencils in the narrow tray at the front. Wolf heard footsteps in the hall, palmed the fifty, and walked back around the desk, reaching the front just before John Fair entered the room. Wolf turned to face the door.

Fair walked in fast and closed the door, then took a big roundhouse swing at Wolf, catching him in the midsection. Wolf staggered, and on the way down Fair caught him again, this time in the precise location of an earlier injury to the kidney. He was now on the ground and in serious pain.

Fair stepped back, breathing heavily, and rubbed his fist with his hand. He was a lefty. "Your standard alky," he said, "he goes down but he pops right back up. He's loose as a goose, like a jack-in-the-box." He yanked Wolf upright and swung again. This time Wolf saw it coming, could see the determination in his eyes. Wolf failed to avoid the blow but was able to angle himself so that it did slightly less damage.

Fair grunted with the effort and hauled him up again, and Wolf drew his left leg up to ease the sharp stabbing ache in his back as Fair propped him on the wall with his forearm against Wolf's throat.

"Not you, you're a sorry motherfucker. What's your name, and don't give me any of that Wolf crap or whatever cute names you fuckups call yourself."

Wolf tried to speak but couldn't; he made choking noises.

"What is it?" Fair was now raising his voice. This was unexpected; Wolf didn't think he'd shout in this office, and he appeared to be getting more frenzied. Wolf was also surprised that Fair knew his name.

Wolf was not a brave man. He feared the return of the fist.

"Robert Alan Moses," he said, spitting out the sounds from a throat that was almost shut.

Fair jerked himself away, loosing Wolf, who staggered to his knees.

"Get up, you," Fair said. "Get up." He had gone around his desk to the chair side, opened the top drawer and pulled out a pencil and paper.

"Give me your social security number," he said, poised to write.

"What?"

Fair looked up at him with the threat of pain in his eyes.

"078-05-1120," Wolf said hoarsely.

"What? Say it again."

Wolf repeated the number.

Fair hit two buttons on his phone. Static, then a scratchy voice said, "Yes?"

"Horace," Fair said without picking up the receiver.

"Yeah."

"Come in here."

"Where are you?"

Anger: "In my office!"

"Right there, boss."

Wolf knew Horace's arrival couldn't be good, and he would have left had he the strength, but instead spent the better part of the next minute testing the extent of his mobility around the sacroiliac area. It was limited.

The door opened with a delicate touch – Wolf hadn't heard anyone approach – and a very large man filled the doorway.

"Get rid of him," Fair said. Without word or acknowledgment, much as he would have lifted a package, the man gripped Wolf by the upper arms from behind and walked him down the hall, supporting his weight and leaving his feet skimming the ground to connect or not as he chose.

They went to the end of the hall, then through the open double steel doors, past the puff of fabric-softener-sheet-scented air from the laundry, through a bare entryway and out to the back, where he tossed Wolf on the relatively soft surface of the trash piled cornucopia-fashion from a thirty-yard dumpster open at the narrow end.

Wolf had tried to lessen the pain in his back through this walk by raising his leg – it seemed to help – but the casual drop brought it back in all its glory. The world grew bright and winked out, and he was immobile and immersed in sensation until further notice.

When next he opened his eyes, the sky had grown dark. Wolf knew where he was, knew he was in the dumpster, but wanted to take it slow. He would sit amidst the garbage for a few moments while he gathered himself.

He turned his head gingerly; to his left, he saw six connected plastic rings that had once held twelve-ounce bottles of pop, the kind children were once advised to cut open to avoid entangling fish when discarded. Underneath, paper trash and, spilling from a Styrofoam container, a tuna salad mess that smelled remarkably bad.

To his right, a bottle of Wild Turkey whiskey, 750 milliliters, almost full. Almost. The seal was broken, but only a little of the brown liquid was missing; the bottle was full from the shoulder down. In a place like this, that was not too likely. In a place like this, the appearance of an almost-full bottle of hard liquor within arm's reach in the garbage was not an accident.

Wolf looked at the bottle and thought about what its appearance meant next to him on this heap. He felt sore and achy, but that was nothing; it was the sharp stab in his gut when he tried to rise that might be a real problem.

He picked up the bottle and observed it, noting the feel of the slender neck and bulging body under his fingers: it had been a long time.

He twisted the cap, took a whiff, winced, and put it back. It was a harsh smell, and it took him to a bad place. He didn't go to that place anymore. He didn't like it or where it put him. He was Wolf now. He was done with alcohol. He was himself a resident, of the Crossroads Sober Living House. He had not taken a drink in fifteen months and twenty-four days, most recently. They were all good days, because when he woke up in the morning he knew he had been sober. Fifteen months, twenty-four days, and counting. At some point, he would stop counting, but not yet.

But here he was, a stranger in the Promised Land Supportive Living Center. It was full of people, not like him, but like the people he lived with at Crossroads. The people he lived with were not quite like him. They were still struggling. They did not have fifteen months and twenty-four days of sober living.

And these people didn't, either. Some of these people didn't have one day of sober living – they were still boozing, or using. It was just less obvious, easier to get by when you were in supportive living. Easy to live the drinking life when you had help with all of your activities of daily living.

He was cold; the night was chilly. But moving put him in such pain he gave up the effort. The bottle was in his right hand; he twisted the cap off with his left and took a swig. It was bitter, and as the warmth coursed through him and he felt its ease, he took three more swallows in quick succession, each drawing in copious amounts, and with each the taste of the burning liquid was softer and mellower than the last. He breathed deeply, then put the cap back on and set the bottle aside, his extended fingers pushing it just out of reach. He lost himself in blame and regret until he fell asleep in the chill and the stink.

IT WAS FULL DAY WHEN HE NEXT OPENED HIS EYES and was startled to see an outstretched hand in his face. He looked up and saw a woman in a dark suit leaning over him with an expectant expression.

"Hello?" she said, as though it weren't the first time.

"Hello," he replied, and wondered how early (or late) it was. He was reluctant to move, remembering the pain and also the fall from grace the night before. Shame, and guilt.

"I screwed up," he said.

The woman's expression didn't change; she seemed to accept everything and expect nothing.

"Not yet, you haven't," she said. "It depends on whether you get up or not."

She held out her hand again and he took it, and they went through the business of getting him on his feet – the night's passing seemed to have effected some repair. While he steadied himself on the edge of the dumpster, she picked up the whiskey bottle and poured the contents into a sewer grate, throwing it back on the heap when it was empty.

"You're Sheila Geraghty," he said.

"Guilty," she said, as though she meant it. "You okay?"

He found he was, enough to move almost under his own power. She was a large woman, and she put a surprisingly strong grip on his left arm just under the shoulder that helped steady his walk, but he hung back in front of the door.

"I should be on my way," he said. Fair's fist had been like a moving brick wall, and he didn't want to face it again. She apparently understood what he meant.

"Fair is gone today," she said. "You can go in."

She brought him to her office and closed the door, which seemed like another bad idea, but she gave him a cup of water from a cooler against the wall that was cold and refreshing, and aside from the muted ache in his back, he felt better than he had any right to feel. She hung her jacket on a hook and waited for him to drain the cup, then said:

"I can get you a ride to the hospital, but you're on your own once you're there."

"No need. I'll be fine."

"No you won't, but it's your call," she said. "So, Robert Alan Moses, who are you and what are you doing here?"

The latter was a good question, possibly one he should give some thought to himself. Another good question was what she was doing at the Promised Land. He addressed the first question first.

"You got my name."

"So you say. I don't know if it's your name or not," she said.

"He tell you that?"

"No," she said, but didn't elaborate. "You're different. What brings you to the Promised Land?" She sounded as though she saw the humor in the name, and nodded toward Fair's office. "It didn't sound like he was doing an intake interview in there." She looked him over. "No offense, but you've either got too much wrong with you or not enough to be living here."

"Fair came to the Crossroads Sober Living House last week and gave fifty dollars to my friend Jimmy McCourt to fill out a questionnaire with a lot of personal information, including his name and social."

He saw the recognition in her eyes.

"But you know this," he said.

She rose and went to a small coffee tray, making a business out of pouring the stuff out and adding powdered cream and fake sugar. Then she looked at him.

"Coffee?"

"No thanks."

She set the cup on the desk and settled herself heavily. She was a big-boned woman and reminded him of someone very familiar. His sister came to mind, but that wasn't right. Linda was half this woman's girth.

"No, I don't know it," she said. She stirred the gritty-looking liquid until the swirling grains dissolved and its color paled. "But it doesn't surprise me."

"Say what you mean by that," he said.

"Ask me what you want to know."

"This place and these people, they don't make sense," he said. "Not together."

"You think?" she said, and paused a second. "Like the name says, the Promised Land is a supportive living facility. The state developed the supportive living program as an alternative to nursing home care for some low-income people with disabilities. The state also pays us a waiver for services that are not routinely covered." She sounded like she was reading from a book.

"So housekeeping, laundry, meds, recreation – that movie theater down there – these are all covered," she said. "The resident is responsible for paying room and board. And most of them have Social Security or some other benefit that covers that. So that's what everyone's doing here. You understand what I mean? You don't have to be poor to get in here, but you don't have to be rich, either." She shrugged. "There are a few people who pay for the whole thing themselves. It's like a hotel and a nursing home put together." Her words were getting simpler and her tone more patient, like she suspected the notion was too complicated for him.

"So what's gonna happen to my friend Jimmy McCourt?"

She gave a small shrug. "What happens to all the people who give Fair their names and socials. Nothing, unless they show up here looking for a handout or a cut. How did you find us?"

"I saw him make a call from his cell to here."

"Well, that's a first. He usually doesn't get too much pushback from the people at the halfway houses."

He had the feeling she would have used a different term for those people if she hadn't been talking to one of them. She drank some coffee, but then continued right away as he was framing another question.

"You get it, right? If Fair gets your friend's social, or yours, he turns it into the state and collects all the aid money for his stay here. Your friend doesn't have a clue, and if the inspectors come around, there's usually an apartment that's being 'made up' for the newcomer."

"How does he keep the money? Doesn't it come to the center, here?"

She shrugged. "That I don't know. It's a shell game. These people know how to move things around so it winds up in their pocket. Not in mine, I might add."

"Nobody ever comes looking for him?"

"Oh sure," she said. "They do. You'd be surprised. People you wouldn't think could find their own ass with both hands in broad daylight turn up at his office." She noticed his face. "Sorry. I see I've offended you. I'm such a vulgar woman."

"What happens then?"

"Not what happened to you. I've never seen him do that before. He know you?"

"He saw me at the Crossroads."

"Huh. No, usually then Fair puts on his jacket, they go out for a friendly walk, and he gives them the brown paper bag. You know what comes in a brown paper bag. I've never seen a one of them again. You're different that way, too." She gave a single laugh. "You must have surprised the hell out of him."

She took another sip of coffee, then:

"You got thrown in the garbage by Fair's bitch. Horace. I won't apologize for that word, it's what he is." She paused a moment, looking into the distance. "At least he's straight about it, the way he is, I mean. Fair is a slick bastard. It's in their eyes – what they mean to do, and why. Fair tries to hide it, but you can see that, too." She balanced a pen on her middle finger and began tapping the point on the desk. "Man started this place, it was love – of making a difference, not of people. With Fair and Horace, you see it right away – that you are but a thing in their minds, for their purposes, could be love or hate. That's the one you have to look out for. You get a look at his eyes? So you know."

He did.

"So now. What are you going to do?" she said, watching him. "What about Fair? You gonna turn him in? You could."

"Why haven't you?"

"I've got nothing on him. Everything's locked up or in another location."

All this tough-edged patter. She didn't add up, with her hand that stretched out to pull him out of the dumpster.

"Why are you here?" he said.

She got up and refilled her coffee.

"When I signed on – I was here at the beginning, when Vic started this place – I thought it would be wonderful. Fantastic! A bright, cheerful place, all these people who had a really rough ride all their lives, finally a little luck. But they're not happy. I mean the dirt-poor ones, the … well. They're never happy, always complaints, give me this, that, gimme gimme and they live like pigs. No, not everyone," she said with exaggerated patience when she saw his face. "But most."

"And?"

She sat down heavily again and faced him. "And also my brother is here. He's got MS, multiple sclerosis, and he was an alcoholic until five years ago. This is the best place he's ever lived, and that includes our parents' house." She sipped the coffee again, then set it down.

"No, I'm not going to even try to report Fair. I believe Frank's success rides on his residence in this environment that's supportive and where I can keep an eye on him. I don't know what to do about Fair that wouldn't run the risk of pulling this place down and endangering Frank's life, which is for once in a good place. I live in dread of the day they find him out," she said. "So I do nothing. If Fair met with an unfortunate end in a back alley it would make my year.

"What about you? Are you going to report him? And if that's your plan, I ask you not to," she said. "I won't keep you from leaving and I won't hurt you, though I could. I do ask you a favor."

She waited, and he said. "If I can. What is it?"

"Spend the night here."

"Seems like I already did," he said, but she didn't find it funny.

"Stay in that empty apartment. I'll have a bed moved in there," she said. "This place does help people. See what it feels like to live in a decent, clean environment with good food and a nice-looking room just for one day. I helped you up today. Will you do this small thing for me?"

The things were reversed; it was the helping up that was small, and the staying over that was the big thing, or bigger, in any case. But she knew that. It was her way of saying pretty please.

THE NEXT MORNING, HE WALKED THROUGH the barren back entryway, through the double doors and out of the building. He was in the alley, the dumpster of the night before 20 feet to his right. It may have rained in the night. He didn't know. He had slept soundly. But the sky was blue, and the air had a fresh-washed feel.

He had spent the day and the night at the Promised Land, like a person who lived there. When he'd left Sheila Geraghty's office, he'd gone at her behest to the dining room – an airy room with golden yellow walls, with fruit tree blossoms pushing against the windows, clean stone countertops, and a punch-colored fountain drink bubbling in its clear dispenser. He was served bacon and eggs, with a side of hash browns, toast and coffee. Two people joined him at the shiny square table; they talked of this and that.

Later, he made a point of sitting on a couch in the lounge, picking up a newspaper and turning the pages. In both rooms he'd felt exposed, having purposely chosen chairs whose backs were not to the wall.

After that, he'd walked out the door – under the awning, past his fellow residents, and down the street. It was a nice neighborhood. New flowers were poking through the dirt in some front yards. It was a cheerful sight. He'd walked through the neighborhood at leisure, noting the church and the small shop at the corner, then went back to the Center, nothing to have to do but whatever he wanted.

Then, after he'd watched TV, even tried out a computer, he'd gone to the room – his apartment, he'd called it in his mind. It was a room that had a lock, to protect his belongings and his privacy; a man with worker's overalls had found him after breakfast and given him the key.

He'd sat on a chair by the window and spent the rest of the late afternoon looking out in the waning light, watched the patch of grass visible in the yard past the alley go from bright to dark green to gray, saw the half-moon rise, noted the odd walker in the middle of the cobblestones and, later, the cats and the rats scurrying along the edges. Then he went to the door, turned the bolt and got into bed, not having seen or been troubled by Horace or John Fair or Lisa or Sheila.

Now outside the back door, he zipped his jacket and looked to his right down the alley, toward the neighborhood he'd visited the day before. The dumpster was over here, and he noticed right away what Sheila Geraghty must have had to walk the entire perimeter to see when she made a similar discovery coming into the building the other morning – a person, although lying at the far edge of the thing, on the cobblestones in fact, rather than in the cushiony mess in the middle that he had occupied.

He came closer, wondering at the scattered position of the legs and arms past the recumbent head. Then, circling around, he saw the wide gray eyes of Lisa, staring without sight at the sky, head at an impossible angle, resting on a pillow of brushy hair clotted with blood. A small brown paper bag was flattened under her left arm; an empty bottle was leaning some little distance away on the dumpster's sharp rusty edge, several drops of an amber liquid pooled in the bottom corner. Two feet above it, floating lighter than air from their viscous red sticking point on the corroded metal, were two strands of wiry hair, one black and one gray.

Assessing his feelings, he tried for pity, or regret. After all, he was sorry to see it. But Lisa was no innocent. She knew what she was doing. She should have given some thought to the consequences of her actions.

Wolf turned the other way and walked down the alley toward the main thoroughfare. He'd been gone from the Crossroads for two days. He had a hundred dollars in his pocket – the fifty he'd taken from John Fair's drawer, plus the fifty he'd taken from Jimmy. Plenty of money, for anything at all. He had nothing to do, and all day to do it.

"HEY, HEY NOW."

"Don't. Don't!"

"Did you do that? Yes, you did."

The men's voices rose and fell. So loud, except for one, but Wolf made it out:

"'Scuse me, 'scuse me, could I have some more?"

Jaybert was holding out his bowl in his quiet way to no one in particular. He sounded like little Oliver Twist with his gruel, but his eyes were shining like a five-year-old's at Christmas.

"Now Jaybert, don't you be taking more than your share," said the Rev. Clarence. He was trying to sound stern, but his tone was contented and his sentence structure intact. He was wearing for once a brand-new shirt: mostly green plaid with a thin maroon accent on a white background, and new tan chino slacks. He gave a chuckle as he put his spoon into his own bowl to scrape up the last of the ice cream.

"As I recall, didn't you ask us to put the extra in your refrigerator, Rev. Clarence?" Wolf asked. "Do you think we might bring it out?"

"Yes, yes, I recollect myself you're right there, Wolf. Yes," he said. "Why not. Let's have ourselves a real treat."

Wolf brought out another half-gallon – Edy's extra creamy vanilla bean – and pried open the cardboard lid. Bowls were thrust forward from all around.

"Jim, see what a good time everyone is having with your gift."

"What?"

"Remember, the ice cream came out of the twenty the man gave you that day," Wolf said. Twenty or fifty, Jimmy wouldn't know the difference. "You said, 'Let's get some ice cream for everyone with this cash.'"

"Oh, right, yeah. Oh, yeah, I did." Looking pleased to be the men's benefactor.

So the little apartment at the Promised Land was a place where a man could make a good start, they might think, but they would be wrong, at least for Wolf and the other men here. He had spent a fine day and night at the supportive living center, had partaken of all it had to offer, but these were the thoughts that had come welling up unbidden over the long and solitary night: Place like this would mock a man every second of the day. Fellow couldn't be straight in his own mind for trying to live up to the shiny granite countertop, or be worthy of the neat built-in desk. The Crossroads men wouldn't even get as far as trying; the fine things would seep into their bones unawares and make them feel lower than they already did or needed to. And that went for him, too.

He had stopped by Sheila Geraghty's office before he left. The light was on in John Fair's office, but he didn't go that far. He stood at the door and held up the apartment key.

"Thanks," he said, setting it on a file shelf just inside the door.

"Well?"

"I had a good experience," he said.

"That's not what I mean, and you know it," she said.

He stepped into the office and pitched his voice slightly lower.

"The social security number I gave Fair is a ringer," he said. "It's a dummy number used to be used on cards sold with wallets so people would know the wallet fit such a card, but some people took it for their own by mistake. Soon as it runs through their system, they'll be on it and be down here digging around. They'll get just him, no one else."

She gave him an unbelieving and troubled stare.

"Now you've done it," she said. "They'll shut us down."

"No. I made a call, see. Wouldn't call him a friend. He'll see to it Fair's the only one gets picked up. You'll see."

And she had. Two weeks later, two men went into the door just past Sheila Geraghty's office and came out with John Fair positioned between them, walking fast toward the exit. Three weeks later, she told Wolf about it when she showed up in the foyer of the Crossroads Sober Living House and spotted him pushing the wide broom.

"So this is it," she said, looking around. "I was on the money about this place."

"This is it," he said. "Like a seat? There are some chairs in the office."

She ignored this question and gave him a look of expectation, a small smile waiting at the edge of her mouth.

"Wolf, you're my hero. The feds came and got Fair, just like you said."

"Good. He won't be bothering anybody anymore."

"I'm here to offer you a job." She straightened her posture and looked him in the eye. "Come to the Promised Land, Wolf. You can start by doing this," she said, nodding at the broom. "We can work something out later. And room and board. It'll do you good, and my brother too. It would do a whole lot of people over there good to have you around." She spoke as though she were telling him he had won a prize, and waited for his answer.

Wolf was glad for the offer. Sheila Geraghty was trying to do a nice thing, according to her lights. But he knew who she reminded him of now – Sister Mary St. Helen, she of the gimlet eye and the ruler, or book, or paddle swift in retribution. Both well-intended in their way. Both with a personal agenda to which they molded their material at hand, scripture or supportive living center.

He was not a hero. No one could give Wolf a name and tell him what or who he was or wasn't. He knew who he was and where he belonged. He was Wolf now. He was a resident of the Crossroads Sober Living House. He had not taken a drink in three weeks and two days, most recently. They were all good days, because when he woke up in the morning he knew he had been sober. Three weeks, two days, and counting. At some point, he would stop counting, but not yet.

Sally Campbell is a freelance writer who for many years has written textbooks and educational materials primarily in the field of consumer economics. This story is her earliest venture into writing fiction.

First Impressions

By Sally Campbell

KATE STOOD IN PIONEER COURT, not far from where Marilyn Monroe had towered earlier in the year, debating with herself. She had taken more pain than she wanted to admit deciding what to wear and even more time getting ready, belying her wish to seem both interested and nonchalant. Her perfect makeup and favorite perfume did little to boost her confidence. She wore a sleeveless magenta linen dress with a pleated flare to the skirt and walking sandals on freshly pedicured feet. Her dark, slightly unruly hair curled softly around her face. She looked far more attractive than she felt as she stood there fingering the charm on her bracelet.

The bracelet was Conrad's last gift to her before he died. He had made her promise to go on living.

"Promise me," he said, "that you will go on laughing and loving. Do it for me." Her tears fell as she shook her head – it was unthinkable. "Promise me, Kate," he insisted. And she had finally agreed. That was two years ago, and she still could barely cope with his absence. The thought of going on with someone else was easy to push aside. Still, she had promised, and it was time to pick up the pieces of her life. Match.com had been her friend Louise's idea. Kate had her doubts but finally agreed to give it a try.

Why am I really here? she asked herself. *This feels so ridiculous. Here I am, a 57-year-old woman standing amidst this milling crowd like a teenager waiting for a man I've never even seen.* The past two months online gave her a picture of the only man on the Match.com site that she cared to meet. There had been plenty of throwaway responses.

Walt was one of the early responders. In his first email, he told her more than she wanted to know about his health and welfare, including his prostate surgery, after which he assured her that "everything still worked." Enough from him.

Hugh was another. He made it clear that he was looking for a wife and he wanted to find her sooner rather than later. He laid out his qualifications. Basically he wanted a woman who was bright and beautiful with a good sense of humor and her own money. Kate crossed him out without a second email. She was dubious about Match.com, and the very idea of marriage at that point was out of the question.

There were several others who failed to get Kate's attention, and she was about to give up the whole business when she heard from Michael. He had a way with words, and his emails were entertaining. She was pleased when he wrote that he would be in Chicago and suggested they get together after his business meeting at the Tribune Tower. Now, she stood with mixed emotions waiting to meet him.

She reviewed all she knew about Michael Lucas. He was a widower of three years, nice-looking if his picture was any indication, father of a married daughter and a twenty-one-year-old son in graduate school. He had a two-and-a-half-year-old granddaughter and a black lab named Slick. And, most interesting, he wrote for a living. Pretty sketchy, but she was attracted enough to meet him. At the same time she was nervous.

She wondered again why she ever let Louise talk her into this Match.com business. *I must be crazy*, she thought. *What if this guy turns out to be a real jerk, or worse? Conrad, this is your fault. What have you gotten me into?*

MICHAEL LEFT HIS NEW BOSS'S OFFICE and caught the elevator to meet Kate. On the way down he thought back on the few dates his friends set up for him after Sue died. What a disaster, each in a different way. He'd been thrown together with Bill's wife's college roommate, a competent, brassy career type. Her appearance was a touch too perfect and she was far too confident. That was over in one evening he thought would never end.

Then Stu hooked him up with Terry, a bitter divorcée who could only talk about what a heel her husband had been. And there was Alice, who seemed to hang on every word he said and said very few words of her own. Certainly he was ready to meet Kate, but his expectations were intentionally limited.

As he left the Tribune Tower, Michael studied Kate a few moments before he approached her. She was every bit as pretty as her photo. He had looked forward to meeting her, but he certainly was not nervous. For him the whole Match.com experience was research for a story. If he and Kate hit it off, it would be a bonus. Clearly she was the most interesting of his online responders. Her emails were quietly witty, and she seemed both intelligent and well informed. He headed in her direction.

"Hey there," he said.

Kate was startled. The voice was pleasant, both friendly and inviting. She looked up at a handsome man with brown, laughing eyes.

"You look a long way away – come on back," he continued.

"Hey yourself," Kate managed, thinking him not only handsome but animated and interesting.

"You must be Kate."

"Right the first time," she replied with a smile.

"You're much prettier than your picture," he continued. "Funny, people never really look like their pictures. They look better or worse – or just different," he observed. "You definitely outshine your photo."

First red flag, Kate thought, *phony flattery.*

"Thanks, but I think you look very much like your picture." *Which is pretty good,* she thought to herself.

"So, how was your flight?"

"Like clockwork, and I'm in a terrific room at the Ritz with a great view. I just finished my business for the day and now here I am with you and the rest of the day ahead of us. I'm going to like Chicago."

Kate laughed. "You have to live through a Chicago winter to be sure." She dodged a Segway weaving through the crowd.

"I'll chance it." Michael replied. "Listen, Kate, I took a walk early this morning and noticed the cruise boat across the street, the Wendella I think it is. I'm a sucker for anything on water. Would you indulge me? The next cruise leaves in about fifteen minutes, at three o'clock, if I remember right."

"Good idea. I was going to suggest it myself. You won't find a better way to see the riverfront and skyline." Kate was relieved. This would be a fine neutral place to get better acquainted.

Michael took her arm as they crossed Michigan Avenue, dodging a loud group of young boys, passing slower sightseers, almost colliding with a speeding messenger on a bike. The smell of caramel corn filtered through the air from Garrett's popcorn shop. A violinist played a lively medley, his case open next to him with a few bills and coins inviting contributions.

"Nice music," Michael smiled as he added a dollar to the collection.

They climbed aboard the bobbing boat, its motor sputtering and smelling like over-oiled machinery. Michael took her arm to steady her onto the deck.

"Shall we go on top?" he asked. "Looks like a better view."

"You're right, it is a better view." Kate headed for the stairs.

They started up the steps, Kate in the lead. She headed to the front of the boat, passing a mixed collection of touristy passengers of all ages, dressed in everything from frayed jeans or very short shorts and message t-shirts to the studied casual of the suburbanites.

"This okay?" she asked, selecting two seats somewhat removed from other passengers.

"Perfect." They settled in and Michael turned to her. "So, tell me some of what I don't know about you, Kate."

Second red flag, vague personal questions. How do you answer an open-ended question like that? Besides, it sounded like a line he's used before. Kate stalled.

"That's a big question," she hedged. "Can you be a little more specific?"

"Oh, I don't know. How about your weirdest childhood pet or how you like your eggs, or what you like to do on a rainy weekend."

Kate laughed. "I did have a weird pet – a big black rooster named Onyx."

"You're not serious."

"Yes, really. He pecked his way around the yard, sometimes perched on my shoulder – he even came when called. Mom wouldn't let him in the house, so he slept in the garage – roosting on the front bumper of the car."

She laughed again. "Actually, one morning my Dad drove off to work with Onyx still perched on the bumper. Luckily someone stopped him before he drove far. I haven't thought of that in years."

"So, are you a bird lover, or was Onyx a fluke?"

"We fed birds when we lived in the suburbs, but it's hard to warm up to the birds in the city. They're mostly pigeons."

The boat started to move, and the tour guide began her commentary. Kate and Michael only half listened, preferring to talk with each other.

"So, tell me about you – how did you become a writer?"

"Actually I started with communications courses in college and ended up in the creative department of an ad agency in New York. We wrote a lot of copy but no fiction, except to the extent that it was all fiction. On the side I took some writing courses and played with some short stories. A couple of them turned out to be pretty reasonable and I managed to get them published. I think the byline went to my head – I was hooked on fiction."

"But how did you go from there to being a full-time writer? I think you are the first published writer I know."

"It was a gradual process," Michael said. "I couldn't afford to quit my day job. By then Sue and I were married and had the kids. She was teaching but didn't earn enough for us to make it without my steady income. Over time I built up a portfolio and sold a few more stories and some nonfiction pieces. Then I met the publisher of a successful regional magazine. He offered me the opportunity to write a regular features column. Sue and I decided with that and whatever other pieces I could sell along with her income and our savings I could afford to leave the ad business and become a full-time writer."

"Impressive," Kate responded. "So what are you writing now?"

For the first time Michael hesitated, looking uneasy. He frowned momentarily. There didn't seem to be a good way to tell Kate that his next story was about the pros and cons of online dating.

"Actually, I'm working on a feature story for my new job," he said. "I'm not really free to discuss it yet. I'll tell you about it later."

Kate noted his uneasiness, subtle as it was. It piqued her curiosity, but he obviously was not going to say more.

"Well, as long as it's not about online dating," she cautioned.

Michael looked a little startled. Changing the subject, he asked, "Didn't you tell me that you are part owner of an art gallery? That sounds interesting. Tell me a little bit about it."

Wary of the abrupt switch but pleased to discuss the gallery, Kate told him how it started. She was an artist by choice and painted as a hobby when she and Conrad lived in the suburbs. She sold a few paintings, mostly to interested friends. She never seemed able to settle into painting again after Conrad died, but when she moved to the city she worked in the gallery part-time to satisfy her artistic spirit.

She and Audrey, the gallery owner, grew to be good friends and then became co-owners of the gallery. When the financial crisis hit in 2007, Audrey struggled to keep the business going, and Kate offered to sign on as an official partner, bringing in capital to keep things running.

"That sounds like a good deal for both of you. I'd like to see your gallery. When are you open?"

"Someone is there most weekdays from ten to five and Saturdays noon to four. We try to show new local artists at least once a month. You'll have to come to one of our exhibits when you are here."

"I'd really like that," Michael said.

Changing the subject again to another safe topic, he said, "Listen, our guide is talking about the buildings we're passing. Are you familiar with all of these views?"

Kate listened to the guide and added a few comments on the buildings she knew, but she lingered still with his unfinished account about his upcoming article.

Michael noted the shift in her mood. He had not expected to be so attracted to Kate. Now he was surprised by how much he wanted her to like and trust him. They continued to comment on the passing sights as Michael tried to get the conversation back on a more personal note.

"It sounds like you've taken this cruise more than once," he said.

"True," Kate answered with a wistful smile. "We used to take our boys on 'city' tours every summer. This cruise always was a highlight for them – second only to the zoo. Now I only go Sundays on the dog cruises."

"Dog cruises? Really. Tell me about them."

"I forgot you're a dog person," Kate recalled from their e-mails. "On Sunday mornings in the summer they run a dog cruise from the other side of the river. You wouldn't believe the collection of owners with their best friends – everything from fragile aging ladies with Great Danes to weather-beaten cyclists with toy poodles – the variety is really entertaining."

"Sounds a little crazy to me – how do they control the dogs?"

"Actually, for the most part the dogs get along better than the people. Of course all the people are dog lovers, which helps. The funny part is, small dogs rule. I saw a tiny Jack Russell back a serious German Shepherd into a corner – the Shepherd was a wreck trying to get out of the way." Kate laughed at the memory.

"Would you consider inviting a newcomer and his dog on one of your cruises?"

"The cruises are open to everyone," Kate replied, smiling but without commitment. "You have a black lab named Slick, right? A great name for a black lab. I'm sure he would like the cruise, and my Zoë always welcomes company."

A larger boat sped past, leaving them in its wake and the smell of its exhaust. Kate reached out to steady herself as their boat rocked – Michael's hand gripped her arm.

Their boat had come full circle and was returning to the dock. It was close to five o'clock. Kate had enjoyed the cruise and considered whether she wished to continue into the evening or bring this first encounter to a close.

"How about a drink, Kate? I saw a couple of interesting spots from the boat."

Caught in the midst of her indecision, Kate decided to go.

"To be honest, I'm thirsty and a drink sounds good."

"Terrific. Do you have a favorite place or shall we stroll until something looks good?"

"Let's walk. It'll feel good to move after sitting on the boat."

They smelled gas fumes as they left the boat, and Kate caught a slight fishy smell as well. The air cleared as they strolled along the Riverwalk east toward the lake.

Kate began to relax with the rhythm of putting one foot in front of the other. They came to a pub with outdoor seating. Soft guitar music filtered out from inside. A few head-starters were already scattered among the tables.

"How's this look?" Michael asked.

"It's perfect, and I'm ready for a drink," she said, with enthusiasm that surprised her.

They found their way to a table at the outer corner near the walkway. Michael ordered a vodka martini; Kate asked for a rum and soda. When the waitress plopped down a bowl of fresh popcorn, Kate realized she was hungry. Even the beer and hotdogs smelled good.

Their drinks came. Michael looked up with too much sincerity and lifted his glass, "Here's to you, Kate – you make Chicago very appealing."

She lifted her glass, thinking, *There goes the flattery again.* She felt her face flushing.

Sensing her discomfort, Michael said, "Really, I've thoroughly enjoyed the afternoon. I hope I can talk you into walking as far as Millennium Park and then to dinner. I made a reservation at Terzo Piano." He paused. "You wouldn't leave me alone in a strange city, would you?"

"My sense is that you can fend for yourself very well in strange cities," she said with some tartness.

"Ah, but I prefer company. I'd really like you to join me."

Sipping her drink, Kate was feeling relaxed and receptive. "Let's think about dinner later, okay?"

Michael sat back in his chair with an inquisitive expression. "Tell me what you like to do in Chicago, Kate."

She thought for a moment. "You know, it seems like I'm always busy, and the days end before I'm finished with them. But when someone asks me what I've been doing I'm at a loss for an answer. Let's see. I love concerts and the Art Institute. Zoë and I do a lot of walking. Sometimes I take a class at the University of Chicago's downtown campus. I play some bridge and belong to a book club, and I eat out with friends pretty often. There is so much to do. Time is the only enemy."

"You sound like a busy lady. I hope you can fit me in sometimes when I get back to Chicago. Any chance you'd be free for dinner Friday or Saturday evening? I'd really like to see you again before I go back to New York."

"Tomorrow night I am busy. I'll have to let you know about Saturday. My niece is in a tennis tournament and I'm not sure of the timing or the plans following the match. When are you leaving?"

"My flight leaves Sunday noon, and it will take me a week or two in New York to wrap things up before moving to Chicago. I'll hope Saturday works. I'll call you tomorrow to see. If not, let's plan on dinner when I get back."

"That sounds good. I should know about Saturday tomorrow."

"Would you like another drink?"

"No, thanks. Let's walk along the lake to Millennium Park."

Michael paid for their drinks and they continued along the Riverwalk to the lakefront, merging with the pedestrian traffic.

As they walked Michael looked around at the boats moving along the river, the people moving in the other direction, the apartment buildings with potted plants on their balconies and the plantings along the riverfront itself.

"I'm going to like Chicago," he said. "The waterfront, the lake, the architecture, and, on the whole, the people seem friendly."

"It's a great place to live," Kate agreed. "I think you'll like it, too – especially if you live in the city."

"That's my plan. Any advice on location?"

At that moment a child on a Razor scooter collided with Michael, the frazzled mother close behind.

"Tommy, I told you to be careful!" she yelled. "Now see what you've done!" She grabbed the boy by the arm none too gently. "I'm so sorry, sir. Are you okay?"

"No harm done." Michael smiled and addressed Tommy. "Hey there, big guy, that's a great-looking scooter."

"Got it for my birthday," Tommy beamed.

His mother interrupted, "Come along, Tommy – don't bother the nice man."

"No bother. So long, Tommy." Michael waved. Turning to Kate he said, "He reminds me of my son, Joey, with his first two-wheeler – he was so excited."

"You were great with him. His mom is probably still scolding. Are you all right? He really rammed you."

"I'm fine. Where were we?"

"Hmm, I think you were talking about liking Chicago."

"Oh, right, where to live. What would you advise?"

"Well, there are lots of good choices. I like the 'city' city. My place is actually near Millennium Park. You probably should start with a good realtor – someone who knows different areas near the Loop if that's where you wish to be. No doubt your employer can recommend someone."

"You're probably right. I'll give it a try."

Kate looked up, "So, here we are at the BP Bridge that takes us to Millennium Park. Frank Gehry designed this bridge. They say it's an engineering masterpiece."

They started across the bridge and Michael commented, "Pretty impressive. What a great view of the lake and the park and, looking up, oncoming traffic." A crowd of pedestrians was coming toward them.

They worked their way across the bridge, dodging a skateboarder and almost colliding with a biker.

"Is it safe to cross now?" Michael laughed.

"To tell the truth, bikes and skateboards are prohibited on the bridge, but it's hard to patrol. You do have to be careful," Kate said, laughing, as she stepped aside to make room for an old gentleman in a wheelchair, pushed by a young man who appeared to be his grandson giving him a city tour. Next came a double stroller carrying identical twins who looked exactly like their mother. At last the way was clear, and they were on the other side of the bridge.

Kate pointed out the Pritzker Pavilion.

"The Pritzker Pavilion also is a Frank Gehry design, both an architectural and an acoustical triumph. The pavilion seats four thousand and can accommodate another seven thousand in lawn seating. The open-air acoustical canopy makes this one of the most outstanding outdoor concert venues in the world. It's hard to believe you're not in a concert hall when you sit under the stars and listen to the music. This is one of the reasons I like living in the Loop. There are free classical music concerts here all summer. I come often with friends and bring a picnic supper. It's just great."

"I can see the attraction," Michael said. "The concerts sound terrific."

"And here is the 'Bean,'" Kate announced. "People love to see their odd shapes on the shiny surface." She took out her iPhone. "Come, let me get your picture next to the Bean."

"Let's ask someone to take both of us." Michael suggested.

They snagged a willing young man, who took several shots. Thanking him, Kate and Michael walked on toward the Crown Fountain.

Michael looked at her, asking, "So, Kate, have I convinced you to join me for dinner?"

"I have an idea," Kate said. "I'll join you for dinner, but first let me buy you a drink at the University Club. It's just across the street, and the twelfth-floor balcony has the best view in the city of Millennium Park and Lake Michigan."

"Terrific," Michael looked at his watch, "and the timing is just right. It's sixty-thirty now, and dinner reservations are at seven-thirty."

They walked to the University Club, which Kate explained was one of the oldest clubs in the city, established in 1887. With its polished wood paneling and massive staircase, the entrance itself seemed to take them back in time.

"This will be perfect," she said. "The club is one of Chicago's oldest buildings, and the new wing of the Art Institute where we are having dinner is one of the latest. You are covering over two hundred years of Chicago architecture."

They took the elevator to the twelfth-floor gallery, where the hostess greeted Kate warmly. "Good evening, Mrs. Crawford – a table on the balcony?"

"Hello, Susan. Yes, please. We'll just be having cocktails this evening."

"Right. Follow me."

They sat down and Michael looked out. "Wow, this is a spectacular view – a great idea, Kate. Do you come here often?"

"Actually, I do – more than anyone needs to, but I live in the next building, and this is one of my favorite places to come in the summer."

"I can see why," said Michael, looking out over the park.

They both ordered wine, and Michael asked Kate how long she had been a member of the Club. She told him that Conrad had belonged, as had his father. She continued the membership after he died.

At the mention of Conrad, Michael sat back in his chair. Looking at Kate, he said in a soft voice, "Tell me a little about Conrad, Kate. How did you meet?"

Kate's face softened as she thought of Conrad. "He was everything to me," she said. "We met in high school, and he was always looking out for me. A couple of bombastic boys used to harass me on the way home from school. Conrad found out and began walking me home. We started dating, and there never has been anyone else. Conrad always made me feel safe, and I knew I could trust him completely."

She looked at Michael, smiling at the memory.

"That was 40 years ago," she continued. "We were married right after college. Conrad started working at the bank and went to graduate school at night, while I worked in a gallery and took courses at the Art Institute.

"We lived in a coach house on Webster near Lincoln Park. It wasn't much of an apartment, really, but it was a great time for both of us. Not many responsibilities and time to enjoy the city and each other.

"Three years later I was expecting Jacob, and we moved to the suburbs like everyone else. Marcus was born four years later, and we were one of those 'perfect' families. It pretty much continued that way until Conrad's illness. Those were good years. It has taken me a long time for the memories to finally bring more pleasure than pain."

Kate looked away and then back at Michael.

"Tell me about Sue. It must have been a terrible shock to lose her so suddenly."

Michael's face clouded at the memory. He hesitated.

"It was hell, Kate. I was paralyzed by her absence. We were living in Connecticut, a short commute from New York. Every place I went, everything I did, every thought, she was both there and gone. I'd walk into the house and feel suffocated. It was hard to even breathe. It took almost a year before I could write again." He paused. Kate put her hand on his, but said nothing.

Shortly, he continued. "The whole thing was so unreal. When I left town on Monday she was fine. She suffered a cerebral aneurysm, and by Friday she was dead. It came out of nowhere."

"We had been married thirty years. Without Sue, my life seemed pointless. I felt like the best part of me was missing. I was a mess." He paused. "Finally, my kids insisted that I see a therapist, and she helped me crawl out of the hole I was in. I managed to pull myself together, move back to New York, and start writing again. Now I'm at the point where, as you say, the good memories bring more pleasure than pain."

"I'm so sorry, Michael. I can't imagine what it would be like if Conrad had died so suddenly. He was ill for two years, and we both knew it was coming. But even when you're expecting it, death comes as a stranger and a horrific shock."

"So, how was it for you, Kate? I mean after Conrad died?"

"My life felt like a shattered mirror. All the pieces were there except the most important one. I didn't think I'd ever be able to put things together again. I didn't even want to. I just sort of dropped out of the life we had lived. Nothing seemed right anymore. That's why I finally moved to the city, to get a grip, to start a new life." She smiled a rueful smile.

"Looks like that was a good idea. You seem to have a good grip now. Are you ready to go for dinner?"

"Ready and hungry."

They walked across the street to the new wing of the Art Institute and the highly hyped Terzo Piano.

"I'll be interested in your opinion of this restaurant, Michael. It gets mixed reviews but it's one of those places everyone should try at least once. I like it myself."

The hostess greeted them graciously and led them to a table by a floor-to-ceiling window with a nice view. The room was large and over half-full with diners spread out at a comfortable distance from each other.

Michael looked around. "Well, it's certainly white and a little sterile, definitely minimalist. I'd say fitting for the modern wing. What do you think?"

"Basically, I agree with you. It would never be my favorite restaurant, but I still like to come here, I think partly because I love the museum. When you have time you really should see the collections in both the new wing and the original. This is a world-class museum. But you probably are used to that, coming from New York."

"Actually, I do enjoy the museums in New York, but I intend to visit the Art Institute at length as soon as I get settled in Chicago. Perhaps you will join me and point out the highlights."

At this point Kate was relaxed with Michael and really enjoying herself. "I'd love to take you through the museum," she said with some enthusiasm.

The waiter came to their table with menus and asked whether they wished to order cocktails or wine.

"I'm thinking we should order a bottle of wine, okay?" Michael asked Kate. She nodded. He studied the wine list and ordered a bottle of Sancerre. "I think you will like this, Kate. It's a nice wine that seems to go with everything."

The waiter returned with the wine and opened it with a flourish, pouring a small amount in a glass for Michael's approval. He proceeded to pour two glasses and recited the specials for the evening. Both Kate and Michael chose a green salad and the sesame-crusted whitefish.

They sipped their wine and talked of books and movies they did or didn't like, trips they had taken, good things about Chicago, Michael's new job and his moving plans. Their food came and they continued to enjoy some lively conversation, their meal, and the view, which by now included the lights of the city. Time passed quickly. They declined dessert but ordered decaf cappuccino. They finished their coffee, and the waiter presented the check.

They walked out and took the Nichols Bridgeway into Millennium Park for a short evening stroll. Soon Kate realized that she was exhausted. It had been a big day with a fair amount of preliminary stress. Much as she had enjoyed herself, she wished to call it a day. Michael agreed somewhat reluctantly. He walked her to the Legacy, the new luxury apartment building adjacent to the University Club where Kate lived.

"Kate, I really enjoyed today. I'll call you tomorrow to see if you are free for dinner Saturday."

"Good. I need to check with my sister-in-law on their Saturday plans."

Michael kissed her gently before leaving to catch a cab.

KATE ENTERED HER APARTMENT SMILING. She kicked off her shoes and greeted Zoë, who welcomed her with wagging tail and full-body wiggles.

"Well, girl, you would like Michael. Next time I'll introduce you. He's so much fun, easy to talk to, and a dog lover besides. We had a great time together." Zoë placed her paw on Kate's knee as she settled into a comfy chair by the window, remembering the highlights of the day. As she rubbed Zoë's ear she thought to herself, *Yes, it was a great day. Still, it was only one date – too soon to feel like I do.*

Shortly her cell rang.

"Hello?"

"Kate, it's Michael. I had such a good time today, and I really want to see you again. But there is something I need to tell you." He sounded uneasy.

"Yes?"

"You asked about the story I'm writing. Actually, the feature is about online dating. I signed on to Match.com to get some first-hand experience – and it also seemed a good way to meet someone in Chicago. It never occurred to me that I would be so attracted to you…"

Kate felt herself grow rigid. She interrupted.

"I knew this online thing was a mistake," she almost shouted. "But of all the things that could go wrong, ending up as research subject never crossed my mind! I hope you learned all you need to know!" She hung up, regretting that she could not slam down the receiver on a cell.

It rang again almost immediately, and she turned off the phone and stared out the window, feeling duped and disillusioned. Zoë, sensing something wrong, buried her big head in Kate's lap and put a paw on her knee.

"That should teach me a lesson, girl," she said. "We're just fine, the two of us. It's just 'me and my dog' from now on. Who needs a man to mess things up? We'll just settle in and keep life simple."

But Kate was far more disappointed than she wanted to admit. Her anger and hurt soon brought tears. She picked up her shoes and threw them against the wall.

"How could I have been so stupid? What an idiot!" Feeling a downhearted fool, she stomped off to the shower.

THE NEXT WEEK KATE AND ZOË RETURNED from a dog therapy session and the doorman stopped them.

"Mrs. Crawford, I have something for you. I was asked to hand it to you personally." He handed her a large red envelope.

"Thanks, Sam." She took the envelope, collected her mail and took the elevator up to her apartment. Inside she walked out of her shoes and poured a glass of iced tea before she sat down with the mail. After tossing the junk and setting aside a couple of bills, Kate examined the red envelope. No markings. She opened it and peered inside. Michael's article peered back at her. The headline read, "First Rule for Online Romance: Tell the Truth." It was today's edition – first copy out.

Kate's heart jumped as she pulled the article from the envelope. Starting with the first line, "Don't make the same mistake I did…" the story detailed their day together in Chicago. Kate laughed out loud in spite of herself at Michael's telling of their story. She was startled to read the final line, "I hope this public apology will achieve what my private apology did not. I very much want a second chance with my online date."

Attached to the last page was a note:

Kate,

Please accept my apology. I really want to see you again. Let's make a fresh start. I will call you late this afternoon. Please answer.
Michael

She was halfway through her second reading when the phone rang. She picked it up on the first ring.

"Yes, I read it clear to the end." Kate stroked Zoë's ears as she talked. "Yes, it's very good advice, Michael. I was just rereading it when you called. Apology accepted."

"Dinner tonight? At seven?"

Kate looked at her watch. Six o'clock.

"Can we make it seven-thirty?"

"Great. See you then – and Kate, thank you."

Sid Mitchell has served as President and CEO of three academic medical centers, lived in the Middle East, and consulted on healthcare issues throughout the world. Upon retirement he began writing as a hobby. He recently published his first book, Excerpts From an Era and Beyond.

Take Me Out to the Ball Game

By Sid Mitchell

I BEGAN VOLUNTEERING A FEW YEARS AGO, shortly after my retirement as a health care administrator. Stuffing envelopes, going to fires in the middle of the night, and being partnered beside vulgar teenagers fulfilling their community service responsibilities to escape jail was not at all appealing to me. At last, three years later, I discovered what I truly enjoyed: mentoring refugees interested in health careers or who had medical issues but difficulty maneuvering within the bureaucratic system.

I met Khalil in June at the Health Careers booth on World Refugee Day in Humboldt Park a couple of years ago. I had mentored clients from Burma, Sierra Leone, Bhutan, and Iraq. But he was the first Catholic Charities refugee from Afghanistan, and he expressed interest in becoming a hospital administrator. I took a liking to him, maybe because he was different from most of the others. He was very motivated and quite energetic. Since arriving in Chicago he passed his English Proficiency Exam, completed three classes at Truman College, held down two part-time jobs, tutored his two brothers, and assumed the role of father of the house until about six months ago when his father joined the family in Chicago. He was very curious and constantly probing, to the point of sometimes being intrusive. And, he had charisma. Besides being six feet tall, with jet-black hair and the usual Middle Eastern two-day beard, he knew how to turn on the charm.

A few days ago Khalil called to see if I was free on Friday – he had something urgent that he wanted me to do with him. He wouldn't tell me what it was, other than that he didn't want to do it alone. The tone of his voice lacked self-confidence and was indecisive, unlike the Khalil that I knew. When I asked, "Are you in trouble? Is there something wrong?" there was silence. Finally he replied, "Please, go with me."

I left my condo on Delaware Place as I set out to meet with Khalil. I passed the Hancock building before approaching Michigan Avenue. I saw the line forming outside the skyscraper. Although shorter this time, it brought back the memory of Khalil's first visit to downtown Chicago. The first question Khalil ever asked me was, "Do you think it would be as easy to knock down this building as the World Trade Center?" I told him that I didn't know, but I always wondered why he had asked. On that first day, once we had gotten to the observation deck, he didn't get closer than ten feet to the labeled windows. His fear of heights was legitimate, given that he had never been in a building more than four stories tall. On the other hand, I had to pull him away from the Waterworks on Pearson Street. He was engrossed with the operations of the water plant. He asked the tour guide, "How much water does it pump per hour? How many people get water from this site? Is it locked up at night?" Because water was such a scarcity in his tiny village in Afghanistan and because he was seeing for the first time the multicolored, painted water pipes, these questions were quite reasonable – at least that's what I thought at the time. His inquisitive behavior created an excitement that nourished our relationship from the very beginning.

I waited for less than three minutes when the #147 Lake Shore Drive Express stopped in front of the Omega store. Black Friday, something I don't think Khalil ever really understood, caused the bus to be standing-room only; businessmen, school kids, old ladies, shoppers with lots and lots of bags, and me. The ride north seemed different this time as I watched the barreled waves crash against the lake wall while balancing myself with the overhead plastic loop, riffling for a reason why Khalil insisted on my spending the afternoon and evening with him in Rogers Park. After transferring to the #155 at Howard, I exited at Western.

It was like I had never left the Middle East. The dress, the music, and the smells on Devon Avenue brought back memories of my three years of consulting in Jordan, Lebanon, and Egypt. I passed the Zeenat Emporium. Khalil had taken me into the Islamic Book Center on one of my early visits to his neighborhood. I could read no Arabic, Urdu, or whatever the language might have been, and he could read very little English. But together we stood in awe as he read to me from right to left and I read to him from left to right. I vividly remember picking up a children's ABC book; he pointed to the apple and said "red," then to the yellow fruit and said "banana," two of the things I taught him when we visited the Patel Brothers grocery store, where the smell of turmeric and curry competed with the rhythm of the *santoor*.

As I headed toward 6333 N. Artesian Avenue the comfort of commonality among such multiplicity caused me to question why the Middle East is always at war. Two women in black, both pushing a baby carriage, one wearing a pink and the other a gray *hijab*, were accompanied by two men walking in front of them, one with a sleeveless vest covering his Duluth Trading Company flannel shirt and the other in a Kappa Sigma sweatshirt, possibly purchased at the Family Dollar Store down the street. Waiting for the bus where it read "Your Ad on This Bench" were two women in *burkas* with at least five gold bracelets over the black gloves on each of their hands. Next to them stood a fully-bearded man in a kaftan, with his *shtreimel* perfectly positioned on his head and the dangling fringes from his *tzitzit* and *peyot* defining both sides of his face, holding the hand of a young boy with a *yarmulke*. The peaceful diversity was one of the reasons I retired to Chicago.

Khalil greeted me outside before we entered his apartment together. Khalil's mother looked as matronly as ever as she welcomed me with a cup of tea. She is what I think the Virgin Mary might have looked like – meek, loving, and innocent. Her eyes seemed to talk. As her brows raised and lowered and the pupils widened and narrowed, she communicated without saying a word. But the communications this time were of anxiety or fear, not the typical Pakistani face I had seen in the past.

Khalil's father entered with his arm outstretched and gave me the Afghan grip that I had received several times before. He seemed much more reserved and quiet than in the past, and he thanked me for joining Khalil on what he called this "day of decision." They both knew from my facial expression that I was unaware of why I was accompanying Khalil. That is when Khalil's father briefly told me his story.

"I met Khalil's mother on a trip to Karachi. A few months later my best friend joined me for a second visit. Shortly thereafter his mother and I were married and moved into our house in Afghanistan. I kept in good condition the family jewelry store in Jalalabad after my father passed, while Khalil's mother cooked and cleaned for an American family. One night the Taliban took his mother from us. The store was burned, and I fled with Khalil and his brothers to Pakistan. Eventually Khalil's mother escaped from the horrors of evil. We owe everything to her brothers who had connections. We are all saddened that Khalil's mother has been unable to speak since that horrible night. I pray to Allah that she will someday talk again."

My heart was in my throat as I stared into her eyes. She replied with her brows and pupils, "Everything will be OK." Khalil's father smiled, and as Khalil and I got up to leave he whispered to me, "Khalil is lucky to have a best friend, too."

KHALIL AND I LEFT HIS HOUSE, he in his white knitted skullcap that mimicked his puritanical thinking of complex thoughts, and me in my khakis, and headed out for the afternoon. He paused in front of the Sarees and Fabrics store and displayed a questionable smile, something I had seen many times before given his inquisitive nature.

He turned to me and asked, "Which one do you like the best?"

"I guess it depends on the occasion, why do you ask?

Khalil replied, "What if a wedding?"

"I guess, none of them really. In most of the weddings I have attended, the bride wears white."

Khalil pointed to the one furthest to the right. "That is my favorite."

I must admit, it was beautiful, yet moderately unique. The upper yellow chiffon with elaborate gold embroidery, with threads flickering in the sunlight, molted at the waist into a layered, pink silk beauty of distinction. A matching yellow and pink graceful scarf was draped over one shoulder and hung evenly to the level of the bright blue velvet hem, giving the gown a sense of class, as well as the needed weight to hang perfectly balanced. I thought to myself, "A 'wow' statement."

Khalil grinned, "I am going to buy it for my mother. The woman looks just like her." It was then that I noticed for the first time that three of the mannequins were the same, but the one to the far right looked much older, closer to my age.

Khalil was very fond of and quite dependent on his mother. An inseparable bond between the two of them caused Khalil to share a great deal about her to me. Her simple and grounded behavior, especially during his father's erratic episodes, was a quality Khalil coveted. Khalil imagined most women in Chicago to be aloof, uncaring, and very outspoken, characteristics quite the opposite of his mother. I purposely never commented on Khalil's perception of other women.

Without question Khalil's father was the decision-maker of the house. Khalil admired the fact that his father knew exactly what he wanted. Not only was he intelligent, but he was highly motivated and extremely determined. When I asked Khalil, "Is it a matter of past behavior or present survival?" Khalil replied, "I'm not sure, probably a little of both. It is what makes my father, my father." Although they were very opposite in behavior, Khalil's parents seemed to love one another very much.

Khalil began to wring his hands as we exited the CTA bus #22 on Clark Street. As he examined the neighborhood, looking for which direction to turn onto Pratt Boulevard, he explained to me that he had worked with this man at the clinic. On two separate occasions Khalil had joined him and his daughter Kassandra for lunch in the cafeteria. Although she didn't work at the clinic she frequently volunteered in order to practice her English. Khalil had seen neither of them since the man was laid off due to downsizing, but the rumor going around before his departure was "he's connected."

The six-foot iron fence around the complex seemed rather uninviting until Khalil punched in the house number on the voice box and the door swung open. As we entered, I noticed the three surrounding buildings all looked alike except for different window treatments and the number of toys in front of the entrances. As we entered the building on the right, Khalil rang the buzzer on the mailbox labeled "Kamran Khan Rajput," and within seconds I heard the vestibule door unlatch. The two of us proceeded to the first floor. The apartment was open by the time we got to the top of the stairs, and the man greeted us with much enthusiasm, especially happy to see Khalil again. I was invited to sit on the mohair couch next to Khalil, and the hospitality of this Pakistani family was overwhelming: tea, cookies, candy, and fruit. Even though the man's English was not as good as Khalil's, the two of them conversed quite well with one another. I gleaned from the conversation that he was on the verge of getting another job, so I congratulated him. "*Insha'Allah!*" the man replied.

A woman entered in white with all but her face covered. Khalil introduced her to me as Kassandra's mother, a friend of the family while in Pakistan. More tea was served and the candies and fruit were replaced with almonds, pistachios, and pine nuts. Although the mother didn't speak any English she seemed to comprehend the lengthy discussion in its entirety.

Khalil stood to his feet as Kassandra entered in her yellow dress and pink scarf, which caused her blushing face to radiate. Unlike her mother, you could tell she was of thin stature and somewhat on the short side like her father. Her hands were devoid of any jewelry, except for a knotted bracelet that Khalil later learned she had made at a cousin's birthday party.

Khalil turned to me and asked if I minded if the two of them spoke in their native tongue, because Kassandra was embarrassed about her English. Of course I didn't object, and the two of them were in deep conversation for over an hour, which gave me time to catch up on my e-mails and phone messages.

She had a humble disposition, which caused me to like her very much even though I did not understand a word being said. Occasionally she would grin, and on a couple of occasions she even laughed at Khalil's animated behavior. This was the first time while volunteering with refugees that I had been so mesmerized by one's eyes. She had beaming brown eyes with pupils that fixated on Khalil's ever-smiling face. If I had not known better, I would have thought they had been the best of friends for years.

The conversation was interrupted when Kassandra's mother entered the room with a silver-plated platter heaped with *mensaf.* My mouth gaped open in surprise, because this was the first Jordanian lamb stew I had seen since returning to America. Khalil had told Kassandra's father of my Middle East adventure, and so I assumed her mother had made the mensaf for me. Her father showed me how to roll the lamb, rice, and yogurt into a ball and toss it into my mouth, something I had never quite conquered during my three years in Amman.

After we had eaten, Khalil said, "All good things must come to an end," then stood to say his goodbyes in both English and Urdu. A sense of satisfaction, relief, and admiration for one another was expressed on both Khalil and Kassandra's faces as we neared the door.

As we approached the iron fence, the gate was easily opened from the inside. Khalil turned to me as said, "You really liked the *mensaf,* didn't you?"

"It was a real treat, as good as any I have ever eaten."

"Kassandra got up very early this morning to make it for me. She is a great cook, just like my mother."

"For you?" I replied.

"Yes, for me. It's a traditional dish served only on special occasions."

Then he added, "We must rush. We are already late."

I heeded Khalil's command and we hurriedly walked to Ridge Avenue just in time to catch another bus.

SKOKIE IN THE 1960'S HAD THE LARGEST POPULATION of Jews of any suburb of Chicago, but as many moved north it too became integrated with immigrants, mostly from the Middle East and Asia. We walked to the edge of Searle Park, where a woman approached the two of us with no hesitation.

"Welcome. Welcome," she said, reaching her braceleted hand out to shake mine. "I am Homa."

As I responded, Khalil placed his hand over his heart as a sign of blessed welcoming.

Khalil explained to me, "I met Homa a few weeks ago at Truman College."

"Did you complete your class? Medical terminology, wasn't it?" Homa asked as we walked toward Niles Avenue.

"I did. Great class," replied Khalil.

The conversation centered on college and work until we arrived at Homa's home. Upon entering I could not help but notice the organization and appropriateness of everything in it, in much contrast to other refugee homes I had visited. I placed my shoes on the shelf in the entrance hall and hung my coat on the hanger before sitting in the chair next to the magazine rack.

Homa's father entered the living room along with his younger daughter. I waited for Homa's mother to arrive to serve tea, but it seemed different here, maybe more American. Khalil explained to Homa's father that he was working in an orthopedic clinic on Touhy Avenue, mostly repairing wheelchairs and removing casts and....

"You know Homa is going to be a nurse?" her father interrupted.

Khalil replied, "No, I didn't know."

He replied, "Tell him, Homa."

Homa replied meekly yet with great pride, "I got a scholarship to DePaul University."

"Wow, that is great!" exclaimed Khalil, and the two of us showered her with congratulations.

Her father said, "The name Homa means 'phoenix rising'; appropriate, don't you think?"

Homa replied, "It isn't a fully paid scholarship. It will cost more than if I stayed at Truman College. But I wanted my last two years to be at a real university."

I gave her a puzzled look, although Khalil showed little expression. He seemed fixated on the announcement of her becoming a registered nurse.

"I should not have said that, I'm sorry." exclaimed Homa. "What I meant was that I wanted to live on campus, maybe even join a sorority."

Her father shouted, "There is no place in this world for organized and secretive groups. No way are you joining a sorority!"

"Father, this is Chicago, not Kabul," Homa said lovingly and respectfully.

"You know what they did to your mother!" her father screamed out to all of us. "You know what they did to your mother!"

Attempting to change the subject, Khalil said, "So, you want to become an RN. I am sure you will make a great one."

"Khalil, I made a promise as my mother was bleeding in my arms that I would make her proud of me. I want a profession that saves people's lives. I know that would make her proud."

"The goddamn bastards, they should all rot in hell!" her father screamed repeatedly.

Homa's sister jumped to her feet. "Juice anybody?"

Homa went to the stand under the smart-screen television and handed me three photo albums. "My mother is in some of them," she said.

Like everything else, the photos were organized. They were in chronological order, from years in Afghanistan to just a few weeks ago in Chicago, with dates and detailed descriptions of each picture.

For the next hour, as I studied the history of the Hussaini family, the three of them conversed in Pashto or Dari, I was not sure which, and in English. On occasion they would include me in the conversation, but I tried to be as nonintrusive as possible.

"So, what do you think of Khalil?" her father asked me.

"Homa's mother would have loved him," was my gushing response.

As we got up to say our goodbyes, Homa walked over and grabbed Khalil by the hand. "I wish you the very best in whatever you decide to do," she voiced while looking directly into his exuberant eyes.

"I'm sure we will both be very happy," he said and then went out the door.

While shaking my hand her father whispered into my ear, "I agree, she would have liked Khalil a lot."

IT WAS APPROACHING SIX O'CLOCK before Khalil and I exited the Yellow Line train. He seemed exhausted and displayed a very concerned stare most of the way back. Maybe standing for forty-five minutes was a contributing factor. He said almost nothing as we walked to his three-story apartment building. An Iraqi neighbor whom I had met before came out as we entered. Khalil gave him a high-five, but there was no acknowledgment of my presence. We dragged ourselves to the top floor, but before entering he turned to me.

"Thanks, it really means a lot that you would go with me today. In our culture a man is never to meet with a woman alone, by himself."

"Khalil, the pleasure was all mine. You have a great extended family and friends."

He placed his arm around my shoulder and patted me a couple of times on the back. "You are truly my best friend. You know that, don't you?"

We removed our shoes, and as Khalil was taking out his keys three different latches from the inside were turned and the door opened. His father greeted us, and he too looked tired and stressed. As we entered, his two younger brothers slowly approached and proceeded into the front room. I had sat there before, but it looked different this time. The two couches and coffee table were removed, and several rugs were scattered on the floor. Three men, none whom I had previously met, were resting on rolled up carpets against the wall. Khalil introduced them to me by name only. I later learned they were the brothers of his mother; all were from Pakistan.

Khalil's brother got up and returned with a cup of tea. As I sipped it, realizing nobody else was drinking tea except me, there was total silence. The men seemed to be repositioning themselves on the floor until a circle was formed, which I was a part of. Khalil's father got up in great haste, as if he were on a mission or had forgotten something. Upon returning to the room I saw a revolver in his hand. He pulled back the hammer, separated the barrel from the action, and spun the cylinder several times while counting the bullets inside. The ambiguity of the day with moments of intriguing encounters faded into my frozen state of being. This was my first exposure to a real gun in the house of a refugee. His father proceeded to close the shades on the two windows in the room. The rays sneaking in on the sides of the ill-fitting blinds seemed to focus the light directly onto the revolver.

I turned to Khalil and said, "I don't feel comfortable with a gun in the room. Maybe I should leave."

Although my words were not understood by anybody except Khalil, they were the first uttered after several minutes of silence. Khalil spoke to his father, and the others gestured at once. The gun was removed from the inner circle, and his father placed it under the pillow on which he was sitting. Little had thawed in my state of being, but I felt compelled to stay. For the next thirty minutes there was loud and precipitous dialogue around the circle. Khalil was apparently being questioned by all the men in the room, although his father seemed to be orchestrating the argument. On occasion one of his brothers would say something, then Khalil would chime in, but almost always his father had the last word. Khalil's fatigue that I noticed while walking from the bus had dissipated and was replaced with exuberant energy displayed by facial expressions and multiple hand motions. On two occasions Khalil stood to his feet, pointed directly at his uncles, and shouted something in Arabic before sitting down. The thoughts running through my head caused me for a split second to forget about the revolver protruding beneath the corner of the pillow.

What had Khalil done? Was I a party to something that had happened during the day that was causing such debate? Why was the room darkened? Who were they hiding from? Why the gun? Why did Khalil even invite me?

After several moments of complete silence, Khalil's father stood and approached each of the three men. He held out his hand, and each touched it as in a gesture of consent. He stood before his two younger sons, and they nodded in a form of sanctioning. He then approached Khalil, who had a fearful and questioning look on his face. As Khalil stood, he took his son's head between both hands and pulled it toward his body. Khalil stared into his father's eyes, then kissed his hands and dropped his head in solace. His father walked past me, as if I were a seated ghost, to the table in the hall. I could see the light from the cell phone as he was scrolling through the screens.

The conversation was rather short with the person on the other end doing most of the talking. He brought the cell phone back with him and placed it in his lap as he situated himself on the raised pillow in the circle on the carpets.

The silence embracing the circle of seven would have been abruptly shattered if only my thoughts could have been heard. Notions of terrorism, disbeliefs of cultural norms, and irrational judgments of immigrant placements were bouncing around in my mind of blood-spattered cobwebs. What started out being a day of pure enjoyment with unfamiliar experiences was ending in a state of radical anxiety, absolute fear of the mysterious. It seemed as if the unspoken minutes elapsed into an hour or longer while the room continued to darken and the circle faded into a state of human solitude.

Take me out to the ball game.

Take me out to the ball game.

The ring tone startled all of us. Khalil's father jumped to his feet. With the phone pressed against his ear, he paced around the circle while the others clasped hands. Khalil grabbed mine and his eldest brother's, while his head sunk further into his lap. The Arabic negotiation seemed reverent in nature, almost approaching politeness; an idiosyncrasy in any Arabic discussion.

His father handed his silenced phone to his brother-in-law, and all were staring at him as he bent over and removed the revolver from under the pillow. My heart was racing and I could feel it thumping, trying to get away from what might be happening. I wanted my feet to do the same as I looked for the door, but Khalil squeezed my hand even harder, forcing me to stay seated next to him. He went to the window and raised the blind. It was dark outside, even more so than in the room. His father opened the window, got on his knees, and with the revolver pointing to the sky fired it six times.

Bang! Bang! Bang! Bang! Bang! Bang!

Except for me, all the others jumped to their feet. Khalil and his father were the first to embrace. His brothers fist-bumped him, and he patted each on their heads and then pulled their bodies into a three-man hug. His uncles held him tight and pounded him on his back as if to say, "Well done." His father then turned on some Arabic music and the dancing began, as did the sirens outside. I continued to sit in full disbelief and total confusion.

Khalil, with a smile on his face bigger than what I had ever seen before and many times more excited than when he saw the painted water pipes, put his arms around me and whispered into my ear. "Her father approved and an agreement has been reached."

I embraced him, equally as hard as any of the others, realizing how fortunate I was to have been included in such an important event. I whispered into Khalil's ear, "Your mother will look beautiful in the gown."

Allyson Lang is a librarian and freelance writer in Chicago. She lives in the Lakeview neighborhood with her husband and two daughters and writes at NorthsideFour.blogspot.com.

No Taste for Chocolate

By Allyson Lang

HE LOOKED AT THE WAITER. "Chocolate. The most elaborate chocolate-filled thing you have." And he smiled at her, knowingly. It was the smile that had kept her across the table for so long.

"You know, nothing for me, thank you," she said, shaking her head.

The waiter turned, but Jeff stopped him. "Come on, let's share something, it's your birthday."

The problem was that she didn't like chocolate, she never really had, but he did.

IT WAS HER BIRTHDAY, 26, and it had been a very nice dinner, but all she really wanted was to go home and crawl into bed. A perfect birthday celebration was drinks with her girlfriends or dinner with family, but not this cavernous and loud New York import restaurant, full of people who looked like they never enjoyed pasta.

They had been together for several years, having met at a lecture at the Chicago History Museum when she was in graduate school at DePaul. He was an attorney, recently out of school, working as an associate at a big firm downtown. Bob Woodward was the speaker, one of her favorites, and she had read *All the President's Men* one more time before the lecture, just to be prepared. Jeff's seat was one removed from hers, and once Woodward started, they both put their coats on the empty seat between them.

Their hands touched when they reached for those coats and they exchanged pleasantries, but Emily was in a hurry, meeting friends at Bricks for dinner after the lecture. Jeff followed her out and offered to help her with her coat, but she hurried past and was quickly out the door onto a busy Clark Street.

"Woodward was great," she explained to her friends, "but the guy next to me was on his phone the entire time. It was distracting, annoying…I hate those things." She settled back for the usual ridiculing from her more tech-savvy friends, the ones she loved but who would have never dreamed of spending an evening listening to a lecture at the History Museum.

Four days later she looked up from her book to see him standing not more than three people away from her on the train. Freakishly small world, she thought to herself and went back to her book. Two stops later he was in front of her. "I would have suspected something more political in nature," he said, nodding to her book selection, *Northanger Abbey*. She smiled, the woman in the seat next to her moved for the door, and he sat down.

"I never really understood Jane Austen, although I haven't read much, only what was required really." He introduced himself, Jeff Carello.

They talked through four more stops, and he did not once take out his phone. This, combined with a great smile and a very animated way of talking, made her sad to see her Fullerton stop. He was going farther north, to meet his sister for dinner in Lincoln Square, which sounded far more appealing than delivery from Penny's Noodles and another night of writing. She gave him her email address.

JEFF'S NUDGE OF HER FOOT UNDER THE TABLE brought her back to this place, this dinner. The waiter hesitated while Jeff tried to entice her.

"Come on Emily, treat yourself. You don't even eat meat – have some dessert!" He was teasing now. But she didn't like meat, and she didn't like chocolate.

"How about this?" he waved at the menu. "I don't have any idea what it is, Fondente with Chocolate Sauce and Peppermint Gelato. You like peppermint. Come on, you can run tomorrow, let's celebrate!"

He nodded to the waiter, who turned back toward the kitchen. He was right, it was her birthday, but maybe this one time he could have ordered a lemon tart, something with fruit, something she really enjoyed.

THE FIRST TIME THEY HAD DINNER TOGETHER had also been at an Italian place, but not this one. They exchanged emails for a few days before he suggested they get together. The banter had been witty; he was smart and just a little bit silly. She appreciated his attention, thought perhaps she had been too quick to judge, and agreed to dinner. At her suggestion, they met at a small neighborhood place near her apartment. Owned by a husband and wife, the restaurant was a fixture on this stretch of Webster, loved for years for wonderful homemade pasta and the genuine warmth of its owners. It was one of Emily's favorite places in the city and she thought it a perfect choice for a first date.

Over big bowls of pasta she learned that Jeff had grown up in Hinsdale, where his parents still lived. He had two sisters, both older, both married. He'd gone to school at Notre Dame, and then law school at Michigan. He loved golf and played almost every weekend in the summer with his dad. His office was on LaSalle, he lived in River North, and he worked primarily in medical malpractice.

Being naturally a bit queasy, vivid details of the rather gruesome case he was working on were not exactly the dinner conversation Emily was hoping for, but he was easy to talk to and comfortable to be with. It had started to snow during dinner, and the view from the front window was beautiful.

Once outside Emily suggested a walk, but he resisted. "Too cold," he complained, then immediately flagged a taxi. One of the best parts of living in the city, she thought, was the walk home after dinner; the opportunity to stretch, peek in store windows, and breathe the city air. Jeff opened the back door of the yellow taxi and slid in next to her. He dropped her at her apartment, and just that quickly, their first date was over.

THE NEXT WEEK HE SUGGESTED LUNCH at the Art Institute. She was downtown on Tuesdays for class, in the morning, so they planned to meet at the front, near the lions. This was a perfect choice, one of her favorite spots in the city, and she was thrilled to find this similar interest. He was a few minutes late, which allowed her some time to wander the gift shop before he arrived. They walked upstairs, to the new restaurant in the modern wing that had amazing views and an equally satisfying meal. He had never been there before and admitted the choice was made by one of the assistants in his office. She asked him to clarify; had he never been to the art museum or never been to the restaurant? She was hoping for the latter.

No, Jeff had never been to the art museum before. "To be perfectly honest, I just don't get it. It's an entire building full of someone else's creativity – why would I want to spend a day looking at that? And everything is either very old or very new, where is the middle-of-the-road stuff?"

Her arugula with pear vinaigrette lost a bit of its flavor as he continued on, fully engaged in a new malpractice case, this time a terribly botched nose job. They walked out the Monroe doors, into a cold and sunny day. He was hurrying to get back for an afternoon deposition and, after a quick hug, he waved a taxi, hopped in and disappeared, without asking if she needed a ride or had plans for the day. She did not have plans nor did she need a ride; she immediately turned and went back in the museum, spending the afternoon enjoying others' creativity.

"COFFEE?" SHE LOOKED UP. The waiter was back: "Miss, would you like coffee with your dessert?"

Before she could answer, Jeff interrupted, "Could I see the wine list please?"

She looked at him like he was crazy; they'd already been through a nice Tuscan red, and now he wanted something else?

"No thanks, nothing for me right now." She shifted in her seat.

But he protested, "Come on, Em, let's celebrate, how about champagne?"

It was often this way, when she was ready to call it a night, to wander home, and he wanted more, just one more drink, one more dance. It used to be that his enthusiasm was exciting, and she usually enjoyed being pushed beyond her normal comfort zone, beyond her self-imposed curfew. Now she was simply ready to go home and a bit tired of always being the party pooper. Did he notice? Had he realized that she was always the one to push to leave?

She smiled resolutely, "All right, how about we compromise, one glass, and yes, champagne, please." And once again she conceded; he looked as happy as she had seen him in months.

DATING JEFF WAS A BIT LIKE LIVING at an all-inclusive Hawaiian resort, on a vacation that never ends. In so many ways he reminded her of Uncle Walt, her dad's brother, a boisterous personality with a take-charge kind of attitude. Jeff chose restaurants, Jeff made weekend plans, and for so long that suited her. When they met, grad school was running her life and Jeff forced her away from her desk, from the books that had become her Saturday evening companions. Her world had been, for almost two years, the neighborhood that surrounded DePaul on the north side, the restaurants and shops within walking distance of her small apartment. Jeff took her north to the Green Mill to listen to jazz late at night and south to Chinatown for Sunday dim sum. He had a plan every weekend; he was her personal tour guide to a city she had called home for 26 years. His exuberance was contagious, but at some point, don't you have to go home? Does anyone really live in Hawaii?

By spring they were soundly a couple. She met his parents in May, although he had wanted her to join them for Easter brunch. Too early, she wasn't ready to share holidays, and she wanted to spend the entire day with her parents. She agreed to a family picnic, on Memorial Day. What she didn't know was that it was an extended family picnic: one set of grandparents, two aunts, one uncle, what seemed like twenty cousins, and neighbors who were, she was told, just like family. Jeff disappeared early, wandering off with a posse of nephews for a game of baseball, and Emily was left with his mother, sisters and assorted female relatives, catching up over gin and tonics on the back patio.

"So remind me again how you two met?" smiled Jeff's oldest sister, Anne.

Happy to be included in the conversation, Emily responded, "At a lecture, at the History Museum, Bob Woodward, one of my favorite writers...," but she was cut off by the shared laughter of the women who had known Jeff for so long.

"Hard to imagine, isn't it? Our Jeff at the History Museum!" His mother and sister sharing a secret that she knew but didn't understand.

She was left alone, to hear about Aunt Matilda's Boston Terrier who was recently diagnosed with diabetes and the ongoing issues with Aunt Kit's cleaning woman and her habit of breaking things. Emily was quiet, not ready to weigh in on the sick dog. In this crowd of women, all so important to Jeff, she felt very alone.

He appeared some time later, invigorated and happy after a few innings, quite pleased to have been on the winning team. His smile was infectious, and, as he wrapped his big arms around her, she was home, enveloped in the good smell of grass and cool spring air that clung to his Michigan T-shirt. When his dad started the grill he was gone again, and so, rather than sit alone, she sought out his mother to offer her help with the meal.

"Oh, please," she insisted. "I told him that he was not to bring you out here and make you work! You are the guest, please sit and get to know everyone. We've heard so much about you, everyone has been dying to meet you! Now, I've got steaks, how do you like yours cooked?"

Emily smiled. Maybe Jeff had forgotten to mention to his mother that she didn't eat meat, but she decided to keep quiet. She picked up a stack of napkins, carried them outside, and sat down again, among the people so eager to get to know her, none of whom turned as she crossed her legs.

THE CLINK OF HER GLASS AS IT HIT THE WOOD TABLE brought Emily back to the bustling restaurant and to this Jeff, sitting across from her, his eyes crinkled from the enormous grin on his warm face. The waiter smiled at Jeff and moved quickly away.

When she reached for her glass, Jeff stopped her. "Wait, we haven't toasted yet." She pulled her hand quickly back to her lap.

"I love you, Em." And she knew that he did but was caught off guard by this unsolicited sentiment.

She smiled. "I love you, too," which came to her easily, as it had for the past few months, without really thinking too much. He reached across the table, and she brought her hand up to meet his.

"We're so good together, it all works so well, don't you think?" He smiled, not really waiting for her answer.

The waiter appeared again, setting down a silver dome in front of her. She looked quizzically at him, and in a slow-motion instant she realized what was happening; Jeff was now to her side, on one knee, grinning from ear to ear. All the buzz from the loud restaurant stopped, and it seemed as if they were the only ones in the gigantic room. The waiter removed the dome and there, in the middle of a beautiful pile of sweet chocolate confection, sat a stunning diamond ring, staring at her from a mound of something she had no taste for at all.

"Marry me, Emily, please, marry me."

She looked at him and knew. The problem was that she had never really liked chocolate.

Mark Bacharach is a gold and platinum smith and has worked for 37 years at his family-owned jewelry store, started by his father in 1944. Mark enjoys cooking, reading about European history, collecting art books and old 78 records, and various forms of exercise. He freely admits he was born much too late.

My Three Bosses

By Mark Bacharach

MY NAME IS MARK, and I am a certified S.O.B. A Son of Bosses.

I worked with both my parents in a family business every day for 27 years until Dad (almost) retired. At various times during each workday, I wanted to quit, commit murder, or administer Chinese water torture. Now that my parents are both gone, and I'm "The Boss," I can better understand how those early years weren't easy on any of us.

I learned almost everything I know about my business from my father. He was the more patient parent; if he had not been, I would not have lasted. Oftentimes it was me who should have been shot or, at the very least, fired.

My father, Leo, immigrated from Germany. He was a superb craftsman, a very skilled gold and platinum smith. In Europe, one needs four years of intense schooling to earn a diploma that certifies one as a master craftsman. The U.S. doesn't require a license at all. Dad's license helped him earn his livelihood as a jeweler, but whether it required a license or not, Dad always seemed to know what he was doing.

He certainly knew what he was doing when he married my mother, Audrey, who had always excelled at any artistic endeavor. She helped design jewelry pieces in the store, and decorated the store and our home. When Mr. and Mrs. Bachrach – the Picky Perfectionist Pair – worked as an artistic team, they were great. They created many lovely things, including me.

As the son of the Picky Perfectionist Pair, how was I supposed to cope with their expectations?

MY PARENTS HAD BOTH EXPERIENCED DIFFICULTIES of kinds I could not imagine. Dad left Nazi Germany at the age of twenty, in 1936. He and his older sister got out, leaving behind their parents and younger sister, whom they never saw again. Dad's first wife abandoned him and my siblings, who were then three and five years old, cleaning him out financially in the process. My mother, twelve years younger than my Dad, lost her father when she was twenty-one, had been through a bad marriage herself, and was never accepted by my sister as "Mom." I was not born into a family of "quitters," and Dad especially always had the unique ability to find the one shining spot amidst a sea of darkness…how was I going to measure up?

Dad wouldn't hear of my moving out of the house until I was settled in my career plans. These took a while to form. So I went from being a know-it-all college graduate to a know-nothing, "go sweep the floor" flunkie, living and working with my parents for four years and paying a nominal rent at home. Dad was a self-made man, and my mother worked quite hard; they were not about to spoil their son. I graduated college on a Friday, took a vacation until the following Tuesday, and then began working in the store where I've been for almost thirty-seven years.

I work late many evenings; sometimes to catch up on things that can't be finished during the day, and sometimes to actually enjoy being alone with my work, which I love. I'm also alone with my thoughts. After nearly thirty-seven years, there are some wonderful memories here; some poignant, a few sad, and others funny as can be. They are different evenings now; my folks aren't here anymore, and Ellen, a close family friend who was my Dad's personal secretary/saleslady for almost thirty years, is retired. I can still talk to her; she is a vigorous and sharp eighty-nine-year-old. Many times I'll bring dinner in and, if there's a problem, I can call and ask Ellen's advice. Sometimes I say to myself, "Now how would we have handled this in the old days?"

Learning a retail business is a challenge under the best of circumstances. Among other things, I had to learn the trade: how to make small talk to customers, how to set up the showcases, how and what types of merchandise to buy. Most important, I had to learn how to keep my sanity while living and working with two people who loved me very much. Each parent had a unique style, and I quickly learned to keep happy whomever was hovering around me at any given moment. Sometimes, however, by making one parent happy, I risked displeasing the other.

For instance, Dad liked many displays in the showcases. My mother felt that "less is more." When he was around me, I'd put more items in the case. If Mom were nearby, I'd take them out. Mom thought that I learned how to set up the cases better than any of the other staff. (Of course I did. Guess who taught me?) If my father was looking disapprovingly at a display, I simply said, "Mom told me to do it this way." Whether or not I was telling the truth, that response always satisfied Dad, and he left it alone. Mom was quite precise in how I displayed the merchandise. If I had three items lined up in a row, she'd scatter them. Once I learned to scatter them, I had to learn how to space them properly. With my parents' differing opinions on display patterns, many was the time that one or the other would move an item by only two or three millimeters; the display had to be perfect.

These many years later, I'd like to think that they still are.

I've written that I had three bosses. Ellen helped to teach me as well. Also a German immigrant, Ellen's life was turned upside down as well. She was the only grandchild (on both sides) of a family that had owned a silk manufacturing firm. Her future had looked bright until, at the age of fifteen, she and her parents left Germany in March of 1939. They went to Havana for six months, then came to the United States. Ellen and her family had left their family business and a large home to settle into a one-room apartment, where the three of them remained for six years until Ellen got married.

She and my father made a good team. Ellen wasn't afraid to let me know when to keep my mouth shut, and she probably saved me from getting a few verbal thrashings...when she didn't want to give me one herself. I found her very easy to work with...except for the time I forgot to mail a bank deposit with several checks. We found it one week later in my briefcase, and Ellen, with a smile on her face, was the first to say that I should have been fired. When my parents went on some business trips and left Ellen in charge of the store (and me), we both worked, and diligently. Even if I'd been tempted to slough off, which wasn't my nature, Ellen would not have allowed that to happen. I came to respect her, and we've been friends for a very long time.

Fortunately, Ellen has always had a good sense of humor (we all did), which she certainly needed when the "exploding faucet" attacked her. Our former store had a sink in the back room, and in old age it became a bit cranky. Sometimes it exploded a bit when turned on, sometimes it didn't. One day it exploded all over a lovely blouse that Ellen wore, and she had to don an apron while letting the blouse dry. Dad was out of the office, and in walked one of our regular customers. Without thinking what I said (the bright college graduate) I turned from the showcase and announced to Ellen, sitting at her desk in the back room, "You'd better put your clothes on, Mr. So and So is here." I can still see her falling onto the top of her desk, exploding in laughter. Mr. So and So wondered if he was interrupting anything...

WE ALL EXPERIENCED FUNNY MOMENTS in very different ways. When I "joined the family firm" in 1977, our business had been going for thirty-three years. Many of the customers were (also) former German citizens who had left because of Hitler. Some had thick accents; some did not. One of the thickest belonged to Mrs. P., an extremely nice, large woman who spoke English with an accent that one could have cut with an axe. She had inherited some earrings that had posts; they were made for pierced ears, which Mrs. P. didn't have. We had to convert them to "French backs," the type that a lady has to twist onto her earlobe. They are also called "screw backs," like a screw with treads on them. My American-born Mom was helping Mrs. P. learn how to twist them onto her earlobes; it had been years since she had worn earrings. She was having a difficult time twisting them on; Mom was patient. Finally Mrs. P. looked at my mother and said, in heavily accented English, "Ach, Mrs. Bach- a- rach, you'd better help me. I haven' t been shcrooving in qvite a few years." My mother, ever the lady, quietly excused herself, went into the back room, and laughed until she had tears in her eyes. I don't remember who finished helping Mrs. P. ...but she got her earrings on.

Yes, my mother was always a lady, with a hilariously funny sense of humor. One night, "The Three B's" were at opening night of the Chicago Symphony Orchestra; I did volunteer work for them, and had to make an appearance. The evening featured a choral selection, and at one point a very healthy diva swept onstage, wearing a magnificent diamond choker. I had never seen anything quite like it and, not having been in business all that long yet, leaned over to Mom and whispered, "Are those real?" Without missing a beat, Mom shot back "Yes. And so are the diamonds."

These situations, and how to handle them, are the things on which business textbooks can't possibly offer advice; it's on-the-spot decision making. I remember the time Mr. J. was with my father in his private office. Mr. J. was choosing a gift for someone who was not his wife. Suddenly Mrs. J. walked into the store to select a gift for her husband. I made some nervous small talk with her. Then I calmly walked into Dad's private office, informed both men (in a high-pitched voice that smacked of emasculation) that Mrs. J. was in the showroom. Mr. J. blanched whiter than snow. My dear old Dad, ever the diplomat, told me to take Mr. J. down the stairs outside of our store. Then Dad went to see Mrs. J., inviting her for a chat and a coffee. Dad was convinced he could get the "coast clear," and he did. I thought he deserved a medal for that one. I don't know if Mr. J. got what he deserved, but *somebody* got a lovely broach from him.

DIFFICULT SITUATIONS LIKE THAT didn't always have such happy endings. Sometimes they were beyond our control. There was the time when we enlarged our store and one of the electricians suspended some halogen lights from a pipe that was hidden above a drop ceiling. Several months later, construction began on a new store next to ours. Evidently "our" pipe was sticking out of the partition, above the drop ceiling, on the other side of the wall. Without looking where the other end of the pipe was connected, the electrician working on the new construction pulled the pipe from his end, sending four of our halogen lights, plus ceiling tiles, crashing down to within two inches of our glass showcases. Moments before this happened, we had two customers standing in that same spot. They had been gone not more than three minutes when the ceiling fell down, narrowly escaping serious injury... or worse. Fortunately, nothing else was broken. The neighbors told me they could hear my angry shouts from three floors away as I ran into the shop under construction.

THESE THINGS WERE SOME OF THE FUNNIER MOMENTS. What wasn't funny was Dad teaching me the bench work. Always good-humored but deadly serious about what he was teaching me, my father was a patient but determined instructor. He taught me the old-fashioned way. For example, when he began his apprenticeship at age fourteen, he did nothing but file straight brass pieces into round rings for a month. One solid month, five and a half days a week. The hardest thing in this trade is to make something either perfectly round, or square. Dad told me that he often came home crying, as he hated it so much. I wouldn't say that I came home crying, nor did I have to do it for a full month...but I learned to hate it, also. And I learned to do it correctly; filing the "old-fashioned way," which meant no wheels or drills (which we have in the shop). No matter how well an item is polished, the final product won't be smooth if the filing isn't. Wavy lines will be seen no matter how brightly polished the item is, and that was strictly *verboten*.

Soldering with a blow torch was next, and this could be fun. If a fly found its way into the workroom, and one of us could manage it, we'd try to "Torch the Fly." And that is how Dad, being fixed up on a blind date, first contacted my mother. He called her on a spring night while he was working on the bench, and also torching flies...six months later they married. Not on the fly...it lasted fifty-six years. I've heard of "carrying a torch" for a person, but not a fly.

Certain solders can be used with certain metals, and (of course) others can't. If one solder has too low a melting point, it can leave a black line after polishing. Soldering platinum was especially tricky as it has a very high melting point, and certain stones can be burned if the wrong solder/metal combination is used. Even though many times Dad would sit beside me and show me how to solder, it took years before I began to feel confident enough to do it without his help. I had to learn how not to burn something. The choice of solder is as important as the choice of metal it will join. Care in applying the solder is absolutely necessary. A silver piece, for example, has to be completely heated all over before the solder will flow; as for gold and platinum, only certain sections need to be heated. It is very easy to melt something accidentally. "Any idiot can make a mistake," my father often told me, giving me a look that left no doubt as to the "idiot" to whom he was referring. "You need to know how to fix it." He also cautioned me, "Think about what you know, and retail clerks don't." Whenever I felt overwhelmed by everything I needed to know, he knew how to encourage me and boost my confidence at the same time.

ANOTHER POINT ON WHICH DAD WAS ADAMANT was that one of a pin not flopping down. The words "pin" and "broach" are used interchangeably by the public; technically, the item is a broach, and the straight pin is what holds the piece in place. The pin is attached to a "joint," and the end, or sharp point, goes into a "catch." A good technician knows how to insert a rivet properly between the two joint pieces, and the pin should be forced down into the catch, with a kind of spring action. The pin falling, or flopping, into place meant that the rivet was too thin.

My father taught me not only how to make the rivet, but also how to make the end of the pin by filing off the end into a precise square so that it offered the "spring" action that was needed. If a pin flopped and there was no resistance, the job was considered a flop. Period. One had to start over and do it correctly.

WHEN I LOOK BACK AT ALL THAT I LEARNED FROM MY FATHER, I wonder where he got all of this knowledge and found the energy to accomplish everything he did. He was only 5'6" tall; I am 6'2". In terms of achievements, I felt pretty small standing next to him. Nor were my mother or Ellen ladies who lightly took the word "no" for an answer. What I learned from all three were not only technical skills; I learned that success, whether it be personal or professional, is a combination of timing, opportunity, skills, persistence, and the ability to laugh at one's self while also learning from one's mistakes. One might say an education unto itself, or unto one's self.

Scott McGarvey has lived and worked in the Chicago area since 1975.
He currently resides along the Chicago River in the Fulton River District.
Scott enjoys the city from multiple perspectives: he frequently sails on Lake
Michigan, kayaks the Chicago River, runs along the Lakefront Trail, and
has photographed many of Chicago's landmarks and skyscrapers.

Three Nights in the Life of Chicago

By Scott McGarvey

One evening a man was walking home from work. He started across the Monroe Street bridge as he had done a hundred times before. But this time he heard a thunderous blast. Startled, he looked down to see a huge barge approaching under the bridge. Then, he noticed the river that the barge was traveling down. The thought crossed his mind that the city he lives in also lives. It pulses and thrives whether we notice or not.

THE WIND IS MY BREATH AS IT BLOWS HOT from the plains and cold from the lake. It serves those who sail my waters and invigorates those who walk my downtown corridors. It howls over the rooftop terraces and through the gargoyles and minarets of my buildings.

MAY 17, 2012 – On this spring night, a photographer checks the lighting as a group of lightly dressed young models pretends to enjoy dinner and drinks on the outdoor Terrace lounge at my tallest residential building. The last rays of daylight warm the nearby skyline. It's one of those May evenings when a stiff breeze off the lake brings a chill to the air. "Say 'Trump Tower,'" the photographer says to his subjects, trying to evoke smiles. The response is half-hearted. "Okay, say 'Hot! Hot!'" he tries. "We're cold, cold!" one girl retaliates. The shutter begins to click as the group relaxes into the situation and, in this way, the next cover of *Chicago* magazine is made.

The river passes below, my veins and my circulation. Seagulls fly along and perch on top of the bridge-houses. Ripples move through my system, driven by the wind, passing by. They reverberate like sound waves from the shores in ever-changing patterns. My channel serves all vessels equally, from kayaks to barges, and it keeps its secrets well. It's murky in color, hiding past experiences that I'd rather forget.

As the sun sets, I foster my denizens in places that are forgotten and overlooked, unnoticed by the hurried masses. A goose sips water from a tiny hole in the pavement of the bike path by the lake. Pigeons find warmth next to the eternal flame in my plaza. Shoots of wild grass peep through tiny holes in my seawall to catch the fading rays. Geese, ducks, and blue herons frolic along my riverbanks. And strollers walk by the last planter in the shadow on the walkway by the river, ignoring the pansies there that are just as bright as all the others, nourished by the love that I send them.

The setting sun brings new life to moments that are frozen in time. Chess masters contemplate their next moves using the playing pieces atop the Wrigley Building. Look away and perhaps one of the pieces will jump over – pawn to bishop 4. Two young guys are locked in a perpetual game of Frisbee in front of the Presidential Towers. Perhaps the guy on the right will finally throw the disc to the guy on the left and then he'll catch it when the lighting is just right and no one is looking – and then hold on to it for a decade or so before tossing it back.

My buildings talk in a slow and permanent conversation –
> *Reaching out to the sky*
> *still awaiting a reply.*
> *If everyone left me alone I would die.*

I don't want to be left alone. So I stretch my tentacles of steel far into the countryside to bring people into my center for a night on the town. I draw them into me. They nourish me even as I harbor them. They are my life and energy. Sometimes I can hear what they say. "Are we really in Chicago?" one boy asks his mom en route from O'Hare. I nod my silent reply.

The afterglow of twilight offers a beautiful luminescence on the windows of my buildings, smoothing my complexion and hiding the ugly rough spots revealed by day. Heavy solid buildings become light, as the rays of the setting sun pass through their translucent sides. The heat of day is retained by evening in a warm purple and red radiance that is my aura.

I feel the pain of wounds I cannot heal. Broken glass on the lakefront bike path stays there forever, kicked here and there by passersby and always a sore spot on my skin.

One such temple of pain is McCormick Place, a big black block of self-isolation. A chill surrounds it even in May as it blocks the sun from the adjacent pathway. Runners and bikers maintain their pace as they pass by. Nobody stops there.

MAY 19, 2012 – On this Saturday evening, the chill there is replaced by a blaze of heat and activity. I hold my breath as armed men set up cordons all around the structure, seize my streets for miles around, and block the circulation in my arteries. People stop in their tracks and the streets empty of all the people who ordinarily walk them. The cool lake breeze loses its life and is replaced by a dry, parched blast. It brings me back to my early childhood when I suffered a near-death experience by fire. I feel my muscles go into spasm as I gasp for breath.

Then I see a large group of people gathering in the West Loop and marching eastward together carrying signs along Lake Street in the twilight.

"Are you from around here?" one young man asks the woman walking beside him.

"No. Guess," she challenges.

"Miami, I suppose, with that suntan."

"No," she laughs, "Harrisburg, Pennsylvania. I just came into town on the bus. How about you?"

"I live just a few blocks from where we are right now. In the Presidential Towers building. Do you have a place to stay?"

"No. I was planning to sleep in the park."

"That might get bad. I've got room in my place. You can come on over when this is done. You can have my bedroom so you'll have privacy. I'll move to the couch in the living room."

They look at each other for a moment and then he continues, "I have to tell you that you look funny in that mask. What's your name?"

And so Ken meets Marge as they walk over the bridge into the Loop. I smile and begin to relax. I have always been a place where people from all over come together, and nobody can take that away from me. And I know the wind and the river will always endure, and my buildings will always reach for the sky.

As I think back, I realize that I've felt pain like this many times and can grow through it, and I reflect on what a long and varied life I've had. I grow in spurts, like the adolescent I am.

I am about change, both the pain and the opportunity. When a bridge is replaced I feel the raw sting as the torches slice through old iron, exposing it to daylight after a hundred years. When a road is rebuilt I recall the decades of memories that have been entombed in the concrete. I also see the light of opportunity as parts of Wacker Drive see the sun for the first time ever. From my childhood, every day I have grown this way and become more aware of myself.

JULY 28, 2012 – It's a warm night, and my awareness is on Lincoln Avenue where something special is happening. The thunder of cars and blaring horns has been replaced tonight by the steps of people dancing at a street festival. I'm rocking to the beat. I don't want the music to end. A singer is performing on the main stage, making rhymes as he goes along based on everyone around him and things he sees going on in the audience. People bop and sway to the music while an older couple makes a valiant attempt to partner-dance. An unofficial entertainer dances in front of the stage, sometimes making obscene body moves to get attention, and solicits spare cash from the audience.

Two girls, without male partners, dance with each other. When the song is done, someone in the band tosses his guitar pick into the crowd and waves, as the band prepares to start the next number. A spirited fan rushes through the crowd to grab the pick the second it lands on the pavement. He looks up and notices the girls. Then, the flash of recognition. "Marge! Hey good to see you. What brings you here?" he asks.

"Ken, hi! Oh, Ken, meet my cousin. This is Diane. I'm visiting her and we're both going to her sister's wedding tomorrow."

They dance as a threesome, talk some more, and then Ken asks Marge if she can break away. Diane agrees and Ken says the night is young and proposes they find something to do. They stroll down Lincoln Avenue with its food stalls and art booths. Then Ken glances at the shelf of a newsstand and notices the *Chicago* magazine.

"Ever been to the Trump Tower?" he asks Marge.

"No," she replies, noticing the cover. "Hey, that looks cool."

"Let's go," Ken encourages. "Let's get away from here."

Marge says goodbye to Diane and promises to meet her later on. And, as the music winds down, I can see that the festival lives on in the happiness of Marge and Ken, bound for the Trump Tower in a nice cozy car on my Red Line, slumped into each other's arms. Perhaps love will grow between them, I tell myself, and the music will never really die as long as they're together.

Actually, when people celebrate on my streets I never let the lights go out completely, because I always remember the traces they leave. The Cows still parade in stains and bolt-holes preserved in my concrete along the lakefront, on Michigan Avenue, and along Wacker Drive. The sculptures outside the Merchandise Mart, long removed from my sidewalks, still show traces of their mounting hardware as people unknowingly step over. My street signs still celebrate the millennium as "Chicago 2001."

I am pain. I am joy. I am love. I am a growing child one-hundred and eighty years old.

I am Chicago.

The man awoke together with Chicago at about 4:30 a.m., as morning's first Green Line train rattled by. As his city reached out and began to draw in its livelihood for another day, the man sat up in bed and realized he would never be alone.

A mother, sister, wife, and grandmother, Barbara Perry worked for many years as a school librarian. She writes and directs children's operettas, attempts poetry, and is working on a novel for kids.

Drake Weekend

By Barbara Perry

LISA WALKED THROUGH THE AMERICAN AIRLINES TERMINAL at La Guardia in her new Prada heels, annoyed at herself for letting her husband talk her into buying them. She liked being taller, but was it worth getting blisters? Her cell phone rang, sounding like an old car horn. She reached into her pocket and pulled it out, dropping a tube of lipstick on the ground.

"Hi, Mark," Lisa said as she leaned down to pick up her lipstick from the filthy floor and wondered if she should throw it away.

"Are you at the gate yet?" her husband asked.

"Almost. Security was really slow." Lisa looked up at water dripping into a trash can on the floor. "This airport is disgusting."

"I thought you'd be used to it by now."

"I'm just dreaming about O'Hare. Oh, shit."

"You okay?"

"I'm fine. I just got to my gate and there's no place to sit. My feet are killing me."

"You'll be fine."

"I know. I'm just nervous about being with my sisters."

"Have a drink on the plane. I'll see you on Sunday. Maybe I'll even pick you up at the airport."

"Okay, thanks. I better go. Love you."

"You too. And don't worry about your sisters. Just go and have a good time."

AS LISA ROLLED HER NEW GREEN SUITCASE down the aisle, it bumped into the first couple of seats. She loved the way the handle swiveled, but she regretted not getting the smaller bag. When she struggled to get her bag into the overhead bin, the man in the seat behind her lifted it into the compartment.

"Thanks," she said. "I really need to get back to the gym or learn to pack lighter." *Back to the gym? Who am I kidding?*

Lisa sat down in her aisle seat so the masses could file past and thanked God and Mark for getting her a first-class ticket. She closed her eyes and took a deep breath, feeling the weight of the script in the bag on her lap. This was it. She was sure of it. After all the crazy plays she'd written that had no meaning to her, or anybody else as it turned out, she'd finally written from her heart. And it wasn't pretty.

A man wearing a suit and tie smiled and squeezed in front of Lisa, sitting next to her by the window. He fastened his seat belt.

"You going home to Chicago?" he asked.

"Yeah," she said instinctively. "I mean, no. I used to live there but now I live in New York. I still feel like I'm going home when I go to Chicago."

"How long have you lived in New York?"

Lisa thought for a second. "It'll be fifteen years this summer. My husband and I moved there just after we got married. What about you?"

"I do a lot of work in New York, but I'll never leave Chicago. You picked a good time of year to visit. The tulips on Michigan Avenue are beautiful."

"I love the spring." Lisa smiled. "Such a hopeful time of year."

She heard her phone ding and pulled it out of her sweater pocket. A text from her sister Jenny.

Change of plans. Friend from IIT invited us all to her apartment for a drink tonight. May include dinner. Abby agrees. You?

Lisa reached down, took off her heels and rubbed her sore feet, cursing Jenny for changing the plans and Mark for insisting she buy these shoes. Lisa thought about their schedule: get settled in their suite at the Drake, have dinner at the Cape Cod Room and drinks at Le Colonial after dinner. Abby and Jenny had asked her what she wanted to do for her birthday weekend in Chicago, and she immediately thought of the Cape Cod Room. She remembered going there with her grandparents years ago: the cozy atmosphere, the Bookbinder's soup. She didn't feel like socializing with Jenny's depressing architect friends. Jenny could see her friends any time. Why did it have to be this weekend?

Sounds great, Lisa texted back with a sigh.

"Bad news?" the man next to her asked.

"Yeah. No. My family can be sort of high maintenance."

The pilot announced their plane was cleared for takeoff. Lisa tightened her seat belt and closed her eyes as they took off for Chicago.

As the plane leveled off, Lisa pulled her bag out from under the seat in front of her and took out her script.

The man asked, "What do you do in New York?"

"I write plays." Lisa liked the sound of that.

The man looked down at the script in her lap, "Oh?"

"Nothing in production yet, but this one may be different." She smoothed the title page with the flat of her hand.

"What's it about?" he asked. "If you don't mind my asking."

"No, that's okay. It's about a girl and her rotten little sisters. Kind of a twist on the old Cinderella story."

"Is that what's taking you to Chicago?

"What?" Lisa thought about her sisters and how they might react to the story. "No, I'm not going to pitch my play. I'm turning forty this month, so my sisters planned a weekend in Chicago. Jenny lives there and Abby lives north of San Francisco."

"That sounds fun. You're meeting in the middle."

"Right. I love Chicago. So much more charming than New York."

"Do you have any kids?" the man asked.

"No. I thought we would. You know, come back to Chicago, buy a house in the suburbs. But that didn't happen. What about you? Do you have a family?"

"I do. Three girls. Two in high school and one in middle school. They're a handful."

"Yeah, I bet," Lisa said, smiling. She thought about when she and Jenny were in high school and Abby was in middle school. All she remembered about her sisters then was how they annoyed her.

"I'll let you get to your work," the man said.

"It's been nice talking to you," Lisa said, a bit sorry their conversation was over. *Sometimes strangers can be so easy to talk to,* she thought. *No baggage.*

FOR MOST OF THE FLIGHT, Lisa read over her script, making notes in the margins. Her seatmate slept most of the way, but as they approached O'Hare, he woke up and looked out the window.

"Take a look," he said.

Lisa leaned over and saw the skyline along Lake Michigan: The Trump Tower, the Hancock building, the Sears Tower. She'd never remember to call it the Willis Tower. She stuffed her script into her bag and got ready to land. She took a deep breath and braced herself for the time with her sisters, hoping their weekend would turn out to be better than their childhood.

LISA PAID THE CABBIE AND WAS GREETED by the Drake doorman, who signaled to a bellman to take her suitcase in for her. She walked up the steps toward the lobby. Distracted by the chandeliers on the ceiling, she bumped right into a man coming from her left.

She dropped her bag and the script fell out onto the floor, along with her cell phone, wallet, lipstick, tampons, a small bottle of lavender oil from her yoga instructor and a quart-size plastic bag of liquids, packed perfectly for this trip. Well, almost perfectly.

"Sorry," the man said as he slipped his cell phone into his pocket. It immediately started ringing.

She looked at his face. "Davy?" She couldn't believe it.

"Lisa?"

Just as she stuck her hand out to shake his, he opened his arms for a hug. They gave each other an awkward half-hug, half-shake, then bent down and started gathering everything that had fallen out of her purse. Davy picked up the script.

"What's this? 'Petite Poise Girls'? Why does that sound familiar to me?"

Stay calm. Breathe.

She'd had a crush on Davy Davidson in fifth grade. Their parents had been in a bridge group and the families had taken a couple of trips together. Now Davy Davidson was Thomas Davidson, playwright, Broadway producer. They didn't run into each other in New York as often as Lisa wished. Her insecurities about her writing – and herself – kept her from hounding him.

Davy handed the script back to Lisa as they stood up.

"Didn't I email you about this? I'm sure I did. You know, it's a little Cinderella story about a girl who is totally ostracized by her perfect younger sisters." She held the script in her hands, wishing he'd take it back from her.

"Ohhh. No, I didn't see it. Who did you send it to? Sometimes my assistant screens things he shouldn't."

"Directly to you, I think." She stuffed it back in her bag, once again.

"Send it to me! It sounds intriguing." He smiled.

Lisa looked down at her aching feet and wondered if Davy really cared about her script. "What are you doing here in Chicago?" she asked.

"There's a reception tonight for Jimmy Slebos. Do you remember him? He went to Franklin, then moved after fifth grade. He's a fiber artist and he's managed to get something into the Art Institute. What about you?"

"Jimmy Slebos. The name is vaguely familiar." *Who was Jimmy Slebos?* "I'm meeting my sisters here for my fortieth birthday."

"A little family reunion, eh? I'm off to one of those this weekend, too. Out in the 'burbs. Lots of family, you know."

"Oh, fun."

All this time, his phone kept ringing and beeping and singing "Somewhere Over the Rainbow" in his jacket pocket.

"Sounds like you're wanted. Nice to see you, Davy. I bet my sisters are around here somewhere." *Where the hell were they?* She glanced around the lobby and didn't see them. Davy's phone kept ringing. "You better answer that."

Davy reached in his pocket and looked at his phone. "Yeah, I guess. Nice to see you…"

Lisa didn't hear him because she was on her way to the reception desk and reaching for her phone. She texted Mark about running into Davy Davidson. Standing in line, Lisa heard the familiar "ah-ooga" of Mark calling.

"So did you ask him about the script?" Mark asked.

"Of course! He said he hadn't seen it but to send it again. He sounded interested. Sort of."

"Good. But can you stop thinking about your script and just enjoy your weekend with your sisters?"

Lisa rolled her eyes. "I guess. If I ever find them."

"You're not with them yet?" Mark asked.

"No, haven't seen them. I thought they'd be waiting with balloons and streamers."

She looked around and saw Lisa and Abby in the corner of the lobby, huddled deep in conversation. Lisa's jaw tightened.

"Oh, there they are. They're not even looking for me. I better go. I'm up next to register. Have a good weekend. Don't forget to get reflexology appointments for us on Monday. My feet are going to need a good massage. I don't know why I let you talk me into these shoes."

"Because you look gorgeous in them. Goodbye, Lisa. Go find your sisters."

THE GIRL AT THE RECEPTION DESK told Lisa that she and her sisters were already checked in.

"Can you give me a key card then?"

"Let's see…" The receptionist clicked on the keyboard. "Looks like they already got one for you, one for each of them, and an extra."

Lisa sighed and turned her back on the receptionist, stumbling over her feet. She looked over to the corner where Abby and Jenny had been, but they were gone. She hid her disappointment and walked up the steps to the Palm Court, past many potted palms, and all the way around the fountain. Spotting the ladies' room in the corner, she knew she'd found them.

Lisa remembered the first time her grandmother had taken her into this ladies' room. "It's the fanciest loo in the city," she had told her. Velvet banquettes, a long line of mirrors, individual stalls with sinks. The height of luxury. Lisa limped down the steps into the room and heard two familiar voices talking at the same time. *Of course.*

"Jenny? Abby?"

"Lisa!" they said in unison.

Jenny stepped out of her stall wearing black pants and a tailored turquoise jacket over a crisp white shirt. Lisa noticed how put together her sister was, but she'd never admit it. Abby stepped out wearing a long black knit skirt, and layers of loose sweaters and scarves. Her relaxed self-confidence bothered Lisa, but she wasn't sure why. Jenny and Abby each gave her a good hug.

"Why are you guys hiding in here? I've been looking all over for you."

Jenny stepped in front of the long mirror. "We haven't been hiding from you." She opened her purse and started digging, pulling out a brush and fluffing her short hair.

"We saw you talking to that guy and figured we had time to go to the bathroom," Abby added. Lisa didn't expect more of an apology and decided to change the subject.

"You look great, Abby. Your hair's gone wild again. I love it," Lisa said.

"Too hard to tame," Abby said as she looked in the mirror. "I decided I couldn't tame the kids *and* my hair."

Lisa thought about Abby and her five kids, about her life in California and how idyllic it seemed. Then Lisa looked over at Jenny, who had gotten out her blush and stood brushing it on her cheeks with great intensity.

"And Jenny, your skin looks great," Lisa said as she wondered if Jenny had gained weight. "I love your jacket. Very professional."

"Thanks." Jenny gave Lisa a smile and kept working on her face. Without taking her eyes off her own face she said, "Those shoes look like they would kill."

"Wow, Lisa! So cute. I could use some new shoes. Maybe we can go over to Nordy's tomorrow," Abby said.

Lisa took off her shoes, with great relief. "But you don't need the height like I do, Abby."

Jenny sprayed her wrist with perfume, then put her comb and makeup back in her bag. "I hope you're okay with the change of plans, Lisa. I cancelled our reservations at the Cape Cod Room. That place is ancient. Filled with old people. Tomorrow night I got us reservations at a new place. You'll love it. The Patels took me there last week."

"The Patels?" Abby said. "Are they the ones you're designing that new house for? You should hear about this family, Lisa." Lisa remembered how much Abby loved listening to Jenny's stories.

Lisa went into a stall, thinking how little she cared about another rich, successful family. "Oh? The Patels?" she feigned interest.

Jenny told them all about Mr. Patel's new startup, Mrs. Patel's medical practice, and their son, who was a sophomore at Harvard.

Lisa came out of the stall and looked at herself in the mirror. Without her shoes, she felt like a midget next to her sisters. She slipped her shoes on, smeared some lipstick on her lips and felt better. "Let's go. Where are we going for cocktails?"

"Do you remember my friend Blake from school?"

"Kind of..." Lisa had no recollection of Blake.

"Was he the guy who drove the old Mustang?" Abby asked.

"How do you remember that?" Lisa asked.

"That's right, a red Mustang convertible." Jenny launched into another story about another impressive friend.

"Let's go see our room and unpack," Lisa cut off Jenny. "I'm not sure I brought the right clothes for this cocktail party."

Jenny led the way back through the Palm Court and the lobby to the elevators. Abby went up to the Georg Jensen jewelry display, just past the elevators.

"Don't you just love these? The lighting is so perfect. And look – that pin is a beetle. Hold on, I want to take a picture."

"What are you collecting now, Abby? Whatever happened to your birdhouse collection?" Jenny asked.

"Same thing that happened to my dolls, teacups, and sugar packet collections," Abby answered.

"You still have your sugar packet collection?" Lisa asked.

"Well, no, I guess the ants found that one. But I still have the others. Some are in the attic, some in the garage." Abby moved closer to the display window. "I'm working on a beetle book. Look at this one! It has the markings of a carpet beetle. Nasty things."

Jenny asked, "Did your bird book ever get published?"

"Yeah, didn't I send you a copy? I might have brought one – I'll look."

While Abby took more pictures of the jewelry with her phone, Jenny texted, and Lisa's feet hurt.

"Did you guys get me a key to the room? Maybe I'll head up. Are we in a suite?" Lisa was ready to lie down. Already she wanted to be alone.

"I'm ready – let's go." Abby tucked her phone in her bag.

Jenny's phone rang as they got in the elevator. "Hi. I'm getting in an elevator so we might cut out. What's up?"

The elevator door closed and Jenny kept talking on the phone.

"What floor?" Lisa asked.

"I don't know. Jenny registered before I got here," Abby said.

"That's NOT what I told him. Is he there? Let me talk to him!" Jenny's whole body stiffened.

The door opened again, still in the lobby, and a well-dressed couple got on and pushed the third-floor button.

"Jeffrey. Jeffrey. Can you hear me? Shit." Jenny looked at her phone and punched call again.

"Jenny, what floor are we on?" Lisa asked as the couple got out on the third floor.

Jenny glanced at Lisa, irritated. "I don't know." She took her phone from her ear and looked at it, then put it back to her ear. "Jeffrey! Can you hear me?"

Abby and Lisa looked at each other. Lisa took off her shoes, put her purse down on the ground, crossed her arms, looked up at the ceiling, and took a deep breath. The elevator went back down to the first floor.

Lisa looked over at Abby as her phone began to ding. "This is Bill," Abby told her as she began texting with her husband.

Two beautiful African-American women stepped into the elevator. One had on four-inch hoop earrings. Were those diamonds? Lisa tried to get Jenny or Abby's attention, half recognizing these large-bosomed women. They rode all the way up to the tenth floor, where these women got off. Jenny and Abby talked and texted as they went down to the first floor again. Lisa put on her shoes, picked up her bag, exited the elevator and walked up to the front desk, this time with more resolve.

A little sweet talk got Lisa her key card and she headed back to the elevator. She saw by the clock above the elevators that it was almost six o'clock, and she wondered if they'd have any time to spruce up before the cocktail party. The same elevator came back but Jenny and Abby weren't in it. She took her shoes off and picked them up as the elevator took her to the tenth floor, walking barefoot to suite 1012. She looked in the open door and saw Abby and Jenny sitting in the two chairs on the platform facing the window overlooking Lake Michigan. They spoke in low tones and didn't look up when Lisa came in the room.

"Where'd you go?" Jenny asked, making Lisa feel like she had done something wrong.

"Did you notice we went up and down on that elevator three times?" Lisa said.

"I think it was only twice," Abby said.

"So what's going on?" Lisa asked as she pulled a straight-back chair next to their wingbacks.

"Oh, Jeffrey's being a pain. I dropped him at Daryl's on the way to the train and now he's trying to get away with murder."

"How can an eight-year-old be a pain? Who's Daryl?"

Jenny and Abby look at each other, then back at Lisa.

Abby stood up. "Jeffrey's almost ten, Lisa. Sounds like you two need to do some catching up. I'm going to go unpack and try to figure out what to wear tonight."

Lisa thought about Jenny's divorce two years ago, how hard she had taken it. Before the divorce, Lisa didn't remember Jenny failing at anything.

"Who's Daryl? Is Jeffrey starting to hang out with a bad crowd?"

"No, Daryl's not Jeffrey's friend. He's my… contractor."

"Your contractor? What's Jeffrey doing with your contractor?"

"Well…" Jenny's phone rang and she picked it up right away. Lisa looked out the window at the whitecaps and the shadows of the buildings on Lake Michigan. To the west she could see dark clouds gathering and wished for a pink sunset.

While Jenny talked on her phone, Lisa got up to unpack her suitcase in the bedroom. Abby had her roller bag open on the luggage rack in front of the closet. Lisa sat on the bed.

"What's going on with Jenny? She was about to tell me about her contractor and her phone rang. Saved by the bell."

"Oh, she'll tell you. She wants to talk about it. She told me in the lobby." Abby stood up and turned toward Lisa. "You think she was about to tell you?"

"Yeah, then her phone rang."

"Daryl is her contractor and they've been going out since Christmas. I guess they've worked together off and on for years," Abby told Lisa.

"So what's the deal with Jeffrey staying with him?"

Abby reached in her suitcase and pulled out another pair of pants and hung them in the closet. Lisa counted the five pairs already hanging.

"Jenny said they've been getting along great. Maybe it has something to do with what she and Daryl told him last night."

"Don't tell me she's getting married?"

Abby came and sat on the bed with Lisa. "She's pregnant," she whispered, eyes wide. "Four months. She just found out. I don't understand why she had to tell Jeffrey so soon."

"The contractor? She's having a baby with the contractor?"

"Yeah. But it's not that bad, Lisa." Abby frowned.

"Well, I don't know this guy, but she can't be very happy about having another baby. I remember when Jeffrey was born, how Jenny used to complain about how much energy he took and how she'd never have another one." Lisa stopped herself. "Well, maybe she wants to be like you and have five perfect kids."

"My kids aren't perfect, Lisa." Abby got up and went back to her suitcase. "And we're talking about Jenny, not me."

"I know. So is she okay with it?" Lisa paused. "Are you having any more kids, Abby?"

"I'm not, no! Bill had a vasectomy. We're done."

"That's good."

For about a minute the room was quiet. Abby kept unpacking and Lisa stood up and looked out the window.

"What are you thinking about, Lisa?"

Lisa sighed and tipped her head back. "Jenny really doesn't like it when things go wrong."

"Well, who does? And she's going to need our support, not our criticism."

Abby continued unloading her suitcase, hanging up dresses, jackets, and blouses.

How did she fit it all in? Lisa wondered.

"I guess I didn't bring my bird book. I'll send you a copy." Abby picked up her purse and pulled out a bag full of colored pencils and Micron pens.

Lisa flopped back on the bed, arms outstretched. "Do we really have to go to this cocktail party?"

"You don't have to go if you don't want to."

Lisa heard Jenny's voice from the doorway. She sat up, feeling guilty, and turned to see Jenny leaning on the doorframe with her arms crossed.

"That was Daryl on the phone. He just dropped Jeffrey off at a friend's for the night. Did you tell her?" Jenny said, looking at Abby.

Lisa felt invisible. "She told me," she said, looking directly at Jenny. "I knew you were about to tell me something."

Jenny's phone rang in the other room. She sighed and groaned. "I'll be right back."

Lisa lay back on the bed and looked up at the light fixture. "Is she going to marry him?"

"I think that's what she wants to talk about this weekend." Abby lay on her stomach on the bed next to Lisa and started sketching the beetle picture from her phone. "Maybe it's time for you and Mark…"

Lisa stretched out her spine and groaned. "My work is my baby. In fact, I'd really like to spend some time working on my script right now."

They heard a knock at the door.

"What's that?" Lisa asked.

"Probably the rollaway. Jenny wanted us all to sleep in the same room. You get to pick if you want to sleep on the rollaway or in the bed with one of us."

Lisa stood up, looked around the room and at the open closet. Abby's clothes filled half of it. Her green roller bag sat by the bedroom door. Jenny's black roller duffle bag and Italian leather purse sat on the floor next to the bed. A big-screen TV hung above the desk.

Jenny came in the room, following the porter who was pushing the rollaway bed. "Put it over there by the bathroom," Jenny told him.

"No. Put it by the window." Lisa crossed her arms. "I'll sleep in it and I want it by the window."

"There's more room by the bathroom, Lisa," Jenny said.

"I don't need a lot of room. I want to be able to sit up and look out at the lights and the lake. And if a storm comes, I want to see the lightning."

ONCE THE BED WAS SET UP, they finished unpacking. Lisa noticed Jenny's expensive-looking clothes and was glad Mark had taken her shopping last week.

"Are we going shopping this weekend?" Abby asked. "I'd really like to get some new shoes."

Lisa looked at Abby's four pairs of shoes in the closet and the ones on her feet.

"I want to get some like yours." Abby eyed Lisa's shoes with envy.

"Are you kidding?" Lisa massaged her left foot.

"We might not have time for shopping, unless maybe on Sunday," Jenny said.

"Did you get tickets to the play I asked you about, Jenny?" It was at a small theatre in Bucktown.

"I tried."

"What? You couldn't get them?" Lisa bristled.

"It's my fault, really." Abby said as she sketched Lisa's shoes. "There's a beetle exhibit at The Field Museum."

"A beetle exhibit? We're going to a beetle exhibit instead of a play?"

"Unless you don't want to. It's just that I never get to Chicago and I need to get some photos of some species that I haven't seen. For my book."

"And I told Abby it would be okay, because I'm sure Mark will bring you back to Chicago to see the play sometime."

Lisa looked at her sisters. The sisters who had planned this birthday weekend for her. She didn't want to go to a cocktail party in a fancy apartment with Jenny's old friends from school. She didn't want to go to The Field Museum to look at bugs. She wanted a cup of Bookbinder's soup and a glass of white wine.

Thunder boomed and made the plate glass window rattle.

"Are we still going to that spa in the morning?" Lisa asked.

"Yeah," Jenny said quickly.

"Of course," Abby added, keeping her face toward Lisa, but shifting her eyes over to Jenny. "You made the reservations, didn't you?"

"I thought you…no problem, I'll call over there right now. I'm sure they can get us in." Jenny looked at her phone. "Ah. It's Daryl. I better get this. Then I'll call the spa and see what we can get for tomorrow." She held the phone to her ear as she turned to walk back to the living room. "Hi, Daryl."

While Abby kept drawing, Lisa got out her script and sat at the desk, determined not to go to that damn cocktail party. She'd go to the Cape Cod Room by herself, come back to the room and watch an old movie.

"What are you working on?" Abby got up and came over to the desk.

"Another script." She never hid her scripts from her sisters, but they never asked to see them either. "Davy Davidson is interested in it."

"Wow! Big-time Broadway producer, Lisa!"

"Who?" Jenny walked in, like a magnet to famous people.

"Davy Davidson. Lisa says he's interested in her play."

"Good for you! What's it about?" Jenny asked.

Lisa squinted her eyes, wondering how to put it. "It's about a family…"

"Oh, Lordy!" Jenny said as she looked at her phone. "It's almost seven o'clock. We have to go. You can tell us about the play while we're getting ready."

"I'm not going. I really don't want to." Lisa said.

Jenny and Abby looked at her.

"Really?" they said simultaneously.

Lisa sat twisted in the desk chair, arms draped around the back, looking at her sisters. Abby and Jenny looked at Lisa, and for the longest span of time that Lisa remembered, Jenny's phone didn't ring. No one said a word.

"You'll have to talk me into it. Who are these people? What's this for?"

Jenny went to her phone and scrolled through her emails. "It's a reception for an artist named…I've got it right here…James Slebos. Fiber artist. Plus, you need to go just to see the art in this apartment."

Lisa squinted her eyes and thought, *James Slebos? Jimmy Slebos? Isn't that the guy Davy said he was going to see?*

"It'll be fun," Jenny and Abby said in unison.

Lisa laughed. "Okay, I'll go."

"All right! Let's get going!" Jenny smiled.

As they got ready to go, they didn't talk about Lisa's play, but instead talked about what to wear, their makeup, and the art in Jenny's friend's apartment. Lisa put on a happy face like she had all her life and tried to get excited about the party. Her new outfit helped.

"So where is this place?" Lisa asked.

"Right next door. We don't even have to go outside."

Lisa looked out the picture window at the dark clouds over the lake. A bolt of lightning lit up the sky.

"That's good."

THE TRIP DOWN TO THE LOBBY was much quicker than the trip up to the room had been. Lisa felt good in a blue and orange jacket over a short puffy skirt. Her wedge sandals were much more comfortable than the heels she'd worn all day. Jenny had on a pale green suit with a lace collar and big white buttons. Abby wore navy pants with an asymetric white blouse and the print scarf she'd bought in San Francisco last weekend. When they got off the elevator, two men stood waiting. One said, "You three girls are gorgeous," which flustered Lisa, making her laugh.

Jenny looked right at him, smiled, and said, "Thanks." She turned to the left, leading them up the stairs. Abby fluffed her hair with hand. Lisa let her sisters' self-assurance wash over her, put her shoulders back, and took a deep, full breath.

At the top of the stairs, they turned right.

"Let's peek in here," Lisa said. The sign on the outside said, The Drake Room. They counted 25 chandeliers and eight gold-wrapped pillars. To the left, a stage was set up for a band. They heard someone coming and turned to go. The two women from the crazy elevator ride met them at the door to the ballroom.

"Excuse us," said the one with the diamond hoop earrings. The sisters stepped aside to let them in and walked out into the hall.

Lisa grabbed her sisters' wrists and pulled them down the hall, toward the apartment building next door.

"Was that..."

"Sh!"

As they went through the door connecting the Drake to the apartment building, Abby and Lisa burst into laughter.

"What? What?" Jenny asked.

Abby knew. "That was Aretha Franklin in those big earrings!"

Lisa knew, too. "I saw her in the elevator earlier, but you guys were...oh, never mind."

AFTER WALKING THROUGH THE CONNECTING DOOR they made their way through a hallway with windows out to an interior courtyard. Another door led to an elevator, and they pushed the up button. A man in a uniform greeted them. Jenny told him whom they were visiting, and he took them up to the sixteenth floor.

Lisa took a deep breath, willing herself to forget that this weekend was supposed to be for her, and hoping to find Davy in order to pitch her script.

Jenny knocked on the brass knocker, and they could hear a pair of heels walking on a wood floor. The door opened and there stood Lisa's best friend from grade school, Claire, who lives in Seattle.

Jenny and Abby took Lisa by the arms and whispered, "Happy birthday" in her ears.

Lisa looked at her two sisters, so confused. "What? I thought this was…"

"Well, you thought wrong," Abby said.

"You didn't really think we were such ugly stepsisters, did you? It's your birthday!" Jenny asked.

Lisa looked over her friend Claire's shoulder and saw a room full of people looking at her and smiling, all people she knew. Mark stepped through the crowd and put his arms around her.

"What's going on?" she whispered.

"It was all Jenny and Abby's idea. I had nothing to do with it," Mark said.

"How…" she began.

A voice came from behind. "Keep going. A lot of people want to see you." Jenny gave Lisa a little push.

"This seems like a dream," Lisa said as she looked around the room and started greeting everyone: Her people, not Jenny's from IIT, but her own friends from school and jobs she'd had, plus her two favorite cousins.

When she got through most of the crowd, she came to another big surprise: Davy Davidson. He looked at her, less awkward this time and said, "I loved your play and want to talk with you about it next week. Did you really have such a rotten childhood?"

Lisa looked at the people who filled the room, then back at Davy. "Well, maybe not so bad."

Mike Pollard is a Chicago builder/developer, a published photographer, and a member of the Nashville Songwriters Association International.

Nice Day for a Blood Test

By Michael K. Pollard

DUMPING THE LAST BAG OF GARBAGE into the steel can, I couldn't help but think what a great day it was going to be. The sun was out, warm but not humid, like most Chicago August days, and I had a day off in the middle of the week. I heard the phone ring in the kitchen, and although I raced up the back stairs to answer it, I debated every step of the way: *Should I or shouldn't I?*

"Hello."

"Yeah, Joey. It's Ted."

"Hey, what's up?"

"What are you doing today?"

"It's my day off. I really didn't have any plans other than taking it easy. Why?"

"Can I come over and talk to you?" He sounded worried. Very atypical for a friend I characterized as Mr. Nonchalant.

"Sure," I said. "Give me 20 minutes."

I hung up the phone, took a quick shower, and while I was drying off, I heard Ted's car in the driveway. I glanced at the small clock on the vanity. *Something must be wrong,* I thought to myself. *He's never on time for anything and yet he's here in 10 minutes flat.*

I OPENED THE BACK DOOR. Ted looked away before stepping in. I guessed he'd been crying. Once inside the kitchen, we sat down at the small oak table, but he still wouldn't look at me.

"What's going on?" I asked.

He whispered, "I fucked up."

Raised eyebrows and a slow "humph" was my initial response. I put one elbow on the table, curling my hand under my chin.

"What happened?"

He tried to take a deep breath but couldn't.

"Jessica's pregnant."

"Jessica. Your waitress?"

He shook his head yes and his lips tightened while he leaned forward. I wondered how he could be so stupid. I knew he had a propensity for women in volume, but I always thought he was smart enough to wear a condom, especially since he had a wife and three kids at home.

Turning sideways in the chair, I thought for sure Ted was going to throw up on the white carpet, but my golden retriever, Grabowski, sat down between Ted's legs and playfully licked the tears off his face. *Well, he has one friend anyway,* I thought.

I KNEW JESSICA THE WAITRESS. I built Ted's restaurant, and since I ate there at least once a week, more often than not I was stuck with her. I didn't like her. To be on the wrong side of Jessica was not pretty. She took offense to everything and was quick to snap back. Especially when you asked her if she was going to write down your order.

One day she replied, "I have a photographic memory!"

"Okay," I replied, barely peering above the top of the menu. "But you still might want to write it down. I'm not sure the chef's a mind reader."

Sure enough, my order for two eggs over medium to hard, fruit instead of potatoes, and regular bacon with whole-wheat toast returned as two too-runny eggs, potatoes piled volcano-high, two sausage patties, and white toast. I wasn't upset. What did upset me was her dropping the plate in front of me with that, "oh, I'm so busy I can't take one extra second and set the plate down properly" sound, followed by the run like hell as she dashed away.

I stared at the plate. I waited. "Where did she go?" I wondered aloud. "I'm not eatin' this." So I read the morning paper and imagined a different headline: YOU CAN'T FIX STUPID!

By the time Jessica returned to ask the obligatory, "Is everything okay?" I tried to soften my reply as best I could.

"It's not what I ordered, Jess."

"Yes it is," she snapped.

"You know," I began to say, "if you wrote it down, we'd have something to debate. But since you didn't, you'll have to take my word for it."

"I have a...."

I raised my hand in protest. "I know, you have a photographic memory."

I skipped breakfast that day and went somewhere else for lunch. I figured her photographic memory would get a good shot of my ass as it was walking out the door. I'm not sure why I was so pissed off, as this wasn't the first time we'd disagreed. And I'm a contractor, for Christ's sake. A *professional* disagreer.

Another day it was the size of the tip I left her. It was never big enough.

Lightning struck again.

"You can really be a prick, you know that, Joey?"

"Jessica, I'm not trying to be a prick. If I were a prick, I'd leave you a buck and some change, then find Ted and tell him to fire you. That's being a prick."

"Ted would never fire me!"

I left Jessica standing in the dining room.

Entering the small back office, peering past storage racks filled with everything from spice catalogs to an oversupply of coffee filters, I found Ted on the phone. His hand made duck-quacking signals in the air while he rolled his eyes.

"Finally," Ted said, hanging up the phone. "I saw you having lunch but I had to call this guy. Was everything okay?"

"Not exactly," I replied. "Jessica and I got into it over the amount of tip I left her."

"So what's the problem?"

"She thinks I should have left her more!"

Ted laughed and shook his head from side to side.

"I don't think it's that funny. She seems to think because you and I are friends, she can act any way she pleases."

"That's just Jess being Jess."

"Look," I said. "This is beyond a level of familiarity that I'm comfortable with. But let's forget about me for a second. What if she's talking to other customers like this? What…"

Ted cut me off with a wave of his hand. "She's okay, Joey."

"Fine," I said. "But don't say I didn't warn you."

NOW IT'S A YEAR LATER and my friend has cooked up his own menu. How could you order up a situation like this? Let's see: "Should I have the extra-deep-fried, battered and beaten 'Ted with extra Jessica sauce on the side' or the slit-up-the-back, deboned version of 'Ted fresh catch of the day?'" I was hard pressed to determine which one of them was dumber.

"What is it you need from me, Ted?"

"I want you to go downtown with me to the Daley Center and meet the state's attorney. I have to sign a document that says I'm the father."

"How do you know you're the father?" I asked.

"Because Jessica told me."

"Because Jessica told you!"

"Yeah."

"Ted. I know this woman. Do you really believe you're the father because she fuckin' told you? Are you kidding me?"

"No," Ted said. "I know I'm the father."

"Do you really think you're the only guy she's sleeping with?"

He shook his head yes.

"Did you have a blood test?"

"No."

"Well, that's the first thing you should have had done. Did you call a lawyer?"

"No."

"Let's go, Ted. You drive and I'll call my lawyer."

If there were any consolation, it was still a beautiful day and Ted had a convertible. We lowered the top and drove down the block. I'm sure a neighbor or two heard me yelling into my phone to Bob, my attorney.

"I know this broad and she's probably slept with a thousand guys!"

Bob replied, "It's probably too late to do anything."

"Well, I got an idea," I said, knowing Ted was listening to every word. "When we get to the Daley Center I'll break his hands and then he won't be able to sign shit!"

Bob laughed. "That might work. I'll see you."

"What'd he say?" Ted asked.

"He said you're fucked and don't sign anything."

"The state's attorney is gonna be really pissed. I promised her I'd sign off today!"

"Fuck her, Ted. Is she going to pay for this kid? No. You are! And you don't even know if you're the father, for Christ's sake!"

"I know I am."

"Would you stop," I said. "You don't know that for a fact. If you keep this victim shit up you might as well pull over, let me out of the car, and go drive into a guardrail or something. If nothing else maybe your wife can collect on the life insurance!"

I had known Ted's wife, Farah, for as long as I'd known Ted, and over ten years we had developed a great friendship. The three of us had started our businesses at nearly the same time. Either one of them might call me out of the blue and say, "Hey, we want to open another restaurant," to which I'd respond by laughing, acting as though I were too busy to work for them, but in seconds I would acquiesce and reply, "Hey, I wanna build you one!" It didn't take me long to figure out Ted was a player. Farah knew it, and she tolerated it to a point. I suppose that's why she tortured him so every chance she got. This was going to break her heart. If I had a best woman friend, she was it! We told each other everything, and as protective as I was of her, I couldn't protect her from her husband's stupidity. And I knew this would be the end of their marriage. I felt sad for Farah and angry at Ted.

One night I left him in a bar on Franklin Street with some friends around midnight. When I asked him the next day what time he'd arrived home, he replied, "About four in the morning."

Farah had left his pillow, toothbrush, and toothpaste on the living room couch. Later that same day when she asked me, "Was Ted with you last night?" I answered yes. Technically he was, just not until four in the morning.

But now I felt just as guilty as he was. And I knew how painful being lied to could be, making it that much easier for me to empathize with Farah. All that hurt, all that anger, hiding just below the surface, waiting for that one moment to explode in frustration all over the person you loved and trusted the most in your life. I didn't want that on my conscience.

So I told Ted, "If you ever tell your wife you were with me all night and you were not, I am going to tell her the truth."

He replied "fine," but I had a sense he didn't believe me. This really made me angry. *Too bad for him.* Barely a week had passed when I entered the restaurant and Farah asked me right off, "Was Ted with you last night?"

"No," I said.

"I knew it!"

Farah stepped from behind the bar and waited for Ted to return from the dining room where he was taking an order. I pushed open the pair of swinging doors to the kitchen and looked for a hiding place. I found none, so I figured, *what the hell,* and stood as close as possible to the crack between the doors. I heard every word.

"You weren't with Joey last night. You're such a liar, Ted!"

"What?"

"You heard me!"

"Well, maybe he's confused…"

Farah interrupted. "Joey is not confused. Don't give me that shit! Who were you with?"

"I wasn't with anyone."

"I know you, Ted. You were sleeping with somebody!"

One of the doors hit me in the head as Ted barged through them. My back was to the refrigerator and Ted pushed me into it before punching me in the left shoulder.

"Are you trying to ruin my fuckin' marriage?" Ted exclaimed while raising his fists.

Both my hands flew up, and I pushed him back against the plate rack in the center of the small kitchen. Three neat stacks of plates fell onto the chef's prep table before crashing to the floor.

"First of all," I said, "the only person ruining your fuckin' marriage is you!"

Overly reactive, perhaps, I reached back and grabbed a butcher knife off the wall rack next to the fridge. "Second of all, DUMB FUCK, if you ever touch me again I'll cut your heart out and drop you before that worthless heart of yours takes one more beat!"

The kitchen staff and Ted stood silent. Except for the sounds of a fryer filled with boiling grease fat, an old freezer's annoying hum, and a warbling refrigerator on its third compressor, there was nothing more to be said. I slid the knife back into its place on the rack.

"Dumb ass," I said as I turned and exited through the double doors.

"I'm sorry," Farah said as I passed her standing at the end of the bar.

"Farah, you have nothing to be sorry for. This guy just doesn't get it. I gotta go."

I went straight home. I'd barely closed the front door when my wife, Marie, asked, "What's wrong?"

I told her the story. She had one comment: "What an asshole!"

But he was such a likeable asshole. I suppose if you had to have a scoundrel for a friend, Ted was it. Eventually I forgave him for hitting me. I figured I evened it up anyway and doubted he would ever try that again, not if there were any knives close by. Ted and Farah began to try to work things out, or so I thought, while Ted and I got back to planning his next restaurant – where he would eventually meet Jessica a year later.

"I WANT TO KILL MYSELF," Ted said as he continued driving east on the Eisenhower expressway toward downtown.

"Yeah, well, don't do it with me in the car," I said unsympathetically. "Why don't you do it at home in the bathtub? Less mess for Farah to clean up."

Ted said nothing.

"Sorry," I said. "Just kidding."

But not really, I thought to myself, mad at his indiscretion.

The courtroom was wide and modern in appearance and probably accommodated fifty people or so. There was no majesty to it. It was unlike any of the older courtrooms in the city of Chicago. There was no sense of significance for what was about to occur or had occurred over time. No. It seemed like a legal revenue factory, and I imagined one person after another approaching the bench and being pronounced, "Guilty, guilty, and *more* guilty."

Was that possible? Could you be more guilty, I wondered? *Only if you were Ted or had a Jewish mother, I thought.*

The courtroom doors closed behind us, and countless rows ahead stood the state's attorney in front of the judge's bench. Whoa! She looked way hot! I wondered how many accused threw themselves at her feet saying, "Yes, of course I'm guilty. Punish me!" Tempted though I was to ask for her phone number, this was not the time. And, after all, I did have a wife at home...but God, she was hot!

"Good morning, Ted," she said with her hand outstretched. "Are you ready to sign?"

Whew, right out of the box! I thought. This woman is determined.

Ted offered some sheepish reply, which I interrupted.

"Excuse me. I don't know why Ted is signing anything. You haven't ascertained that he is, *in fact*, the father."

"No," she replied. "We haven't done that because Mr. Grazer has stipulated that he is, *in fact*, the father."

Note to self, I thought. *Mental foreplay can be fun, too!*

"Regardless," I said, "you didn't do a blood test and no one really knows, *in fact*, if he is the father, and I would suggest before he sign this document, or any other for that matter, we have a blood test done."

That did it! She was pissed. She threw her pen on the desk and turned a shade of red I was not familiar with, although I thought I had seen them all because few men can piss off a woman more than me. She yelled two questions in quick succession.

"Are you Mr. Grazer's attorney?"

"No," I replied.

"Are you an attorney?"

"No."

"Than I'm ordering you to leave this courtroom!"

"Why?" I asked.

"You are not an attorney and there's no reason you should be here."

"I'm his friend."

"Bailiff. Bailiff!" she screamed, as if she'd read my mind and was offended by some perverted thought I had. So much for the mental foreplay.

Bailiffs made their way to me from both directions – big, maybe muscular, but more fat big. As I listened to the sounds of their nightsticks banging against the seats, I turned toward Ted.

"You don't have to sign shit, Ted!"

Then I looked at the state's attorney. My guy thoughts aside, I restated my position. "He has a legal right to a blood test. I may not be an attorney, but I know that!"

Two bailiffs, one under each arm, picked me up and carried me out of the courtroom. Neither of my feet touched the ground as we passed the empty rows of the future guilty. But I knew Ted wasn't. I repeatedly screamed my soon-to-be-infamous last two words.

"Don't sign! Don't sign!"

Each bailiff kicked open an exit door from the pair and set me down outside.

"What about my friend?"

"Look," said one bailiff. "You can't go back in there. We can and will arrest you. He'll be out in a few minutes, so go have a smoke or something."

"I quit," I said.

"Yeah, well, maybe it's time you take it back up again. Just stay outside."

Hoping Ted would see me when he was finished, I took a seat on a stone bench near the courtroom exit door. I didn't wait long. Twenty minutes later, Ted came through the same set of doors.

"So?" I asked.

Ted shook his head. "Let's just go."

We drove west on Washington Street for a block or two before traffic stopped. Ted incessantly ran his hands through his hair. His anxiety was contagious, and I may have done the same because that's what guys often do when they're nervous, even though I don't have any hair.

"I don't know how I'm going to tell Farah," he said. "I know she'll divorce me."

"I'm sorry. Hopefully she won't," I said, but I knew she would. "What did the state's attorney say?"

"She said I have to go to a lab next week for a blood test."

"Okay. So next week you give some blood and we'll see what happens. How do you think you're going to tell Farah?"

"I didn't think I'd get through today," Ted replied. "I guess I'll ask her to go for a walk or maybe take her out to dinner."

"A walk might be safer," I suggested. "If you take her to dinner she might either stick something in you or throw something at you."

"You think?"

"Duh, she's Italian. She'll probably call her father and have you whacked!"

"No, she wouldn't do that," Ted said, looking to me for reassurance.

"I would."

Little else was said as traffic began moving again. I tried to think of something else besides a pregnant waitress with rotten teeth. *What the hell was this guy thinking?* I kept asking myself. But I knew the answer. He wasn't.

"Thanks for going with me," Ted said as we pulled up in front of my house.

"Not a problem," I replied. "I just hope I didn't make things worse with the state's attorney."

"God, what a bitch she was."

"Well, Ted, let's hope you're not the father and leave it at that. Good luck with Farah tonight." I closed the car door and gestured a thumbs-up goodbye.

Marie was home early from work and preparing dinner in the kitchen.

"Did you enjoy your day off, dear?"

"I'm not sure I'd classify today as a day off."

"What's going on?" she asked.

"I spent the day at the Daley Center with Ted. He knocked up his waitress Jessica, or he thinks he did anyway."

"Jessica!" Marie exclaimed. "The ugly one with the rotten teeth?"

I laughed. Marie was never one to mince words.

FARAH CALLED ME SATURDAY AFTERNOON and we agreed to meet at the local Starbucks on Sunday morning at ten. I arrived early, thinking I'd have a chance to read the *Chicago Tribune* and *The New York Times,* but she was already there, seated at a corner table not far from the counter. I waved hello and pointed toward the cashier.

"Do you want anything?"

She shook her head no and pointed at what I guessed was a cup of tea.

I got my coffee and sat down beside her. Her eyes were swollen, red, and sad.

"How could he do this me?" she asked. "We have three beautiful children. What am I supposed to do?"

"I don't know," I said.

"I think I want a divorce. When Ted asked me to go for a walk, I knew something was wrong. We never go for walks. Then he tried to hold my hand. He hasn't held my hand in I don't know how long."

I watched as she took a sip of tea but was not surprised by what she said next.

"I wish they would have cut his dick off that day he went in the hospital and had that wart removed. I'm so damn angry!"

"Well, you certainly have a right to be."

"Do you think Ted's the father?"

"I don't know. I doubt it, to tell you the truth," I said.

"Why?"

"I've seen how Jessica acts in the restaurant. She flirts with every guy who comes in, and it doesn't seem to matter whether they're with someone or not."

"Really?" Farah asked. I nodded yes.

"Well, why did she have to sleep with my husband if she's so preoccupied with all these other men?"

"Who knows?" I replied.

"Did you sleep with her?"

I offered a slight smile of "no regret" before saying, "No. She's hated me ever since I told her my brother was an orthodontist and I could probably get her a discount!"

Farah flashed a small grin. "I think I'm going to kill Ted."

"You're not going to do that. You've got three kids and they need their mother."

"I know," she said. "Would you kill him for me?"

Visions of spending the rest of my life sleeping with a bunch of gangbangers, drug dealers, and child molesters in some nameless downstate Illinois prison didn't appeal to me.

"I told him to do you a favor on the way back from the Daley Center. Go drive into a guardrail or something so you could collect on the life insurance. Seems fair, doesn't it?"

Finally, I had coaxed a small laugh from Farah before she replied, "Yes, except I know we're not up to date on the premiums."

We sat silent for a few moments. Farah turned in her seat toward the corner, away from the other customers like us, and started to cry. I leaned toward her and put my hand on her back.

"I'm not paying for this whore bastard's kid. I'm not, I'm just not," she blurted into a handful of Kleenex.

"It's going to be okay," I said. "I promise."

But I didn't really know.

I knew this was not the time to start pointing out options, not that she had that many. I guessed it was time to do what good friends do best, be quiet and listen.

"I don't know why I've put up with his crap all these years. I really don't. It's so painful. I feel I've spent my entire adult life with someone I don't really know. When I think of all those nights I drove around, looking for him when he didn't come home, imagining him with another woman. My stomach would churn at every couple I'd see coming out of some bar. Eventually I'd give up, go home, and go to bed. I don't know if I've stayed with him because I'm afraid of being alone, because of the kids, or both. I've never felt lonelier than I feel now."

"Listen," I said. "You're not alone. I'm right here. You've always been there for me, and I will be for you."

"Thank you," she said turning back toward the table. "I should go now and let you get on with your day."

"I want you to call me if you hear anything, Farah." I tried to sound as reassuring as I could while getting up from the table.

FOR ME, THE NEXT FEW DAYS flew by. For Farah, I imagined they felt like an eternity. Perhaps for Ted as well, but I didn't really give a shit. Well, really I did, but I didn't want to admit it out of loyalty to Farah.

Not hearing from either Farah or Ted, I decided to go to the restaurant. It was in between lunch and dinner on a Wednesday afternoon, and there wasn't a soul in the place except for two bartenders and the wait staff folding napkins in preparation for the always-hoped-for evening rush. Jessica was long gone. I was happy about that and took a seat at the bar.

"Hey Joey, how you doin'," Sammy the bartender asked. "What can I get you?"

"Ahh, I think I'll have a scotch on the rocks."

"Startin' early today, huh?" he commented.

"Yeah. Hey, is Ted around?"

"He's in the back office. He doesn't seem very happy."

I laid a ten-dollar bill on the bar, took my glass of scotch, and headed for the back. I found Ted with his head down on the desk.

"Ted," I said. "You awake, man?"

His head rose.

"Yeah. Just tired. I haven't been sleeping much."

"Well, I was gettin' worried about you. What's going on?"

"With me and Farah or Jessica?"

"Either or," I replied.

"Well, Farah wants a divorce."

"And…?"

"She told me to fire Jessica, so I did that on Monday."

"How'd that go?" I asked.

"She was pissed. Started cryin' and yellin'. How could I do this to the mother of our child, on and on." Ted waved his hand in a circling motion before raising it to his head in a handgun gesture. "Shoot me now," he said.

"Well, did you get the blood test done?"

"Not yet. I'm going tomorrow morning."

Ted looked liked a deer in the headlights, the kind of deer you always feel sorry for, if you happen to be unfortunate enough to hit one late at night on some back country road. They're a mess, your car's a mess, and then you have to get out and make sure you killed him but you can't get too close. And I wondered if I was too close, but that's what friends are supposed to be, right? And I did tell Farah I wouldn't kill him.

"Do you want me to go with you?" I asked.

"Would you? I have to be at this lab in the city at nine a.m."

"I'll pick you up at eight," I said.

THE NEXT MORNING I WATCHED as Ted grabbed the shaky handrail, making his way down the front stairs. I know he and Farah wanted me to replace the entire stairway, but I was pretty sure this wasn't going to be happening for a while. He opened the car door and plopped himself into the seat next to me.

"You ready for this?" I asked.

"As ready as I'm gonna be. Maybe we should stop for a drink?"

"It's eight o'clock in the morning," I said, stepping on the gas.

"Yeah, well, we started drinkin' at six, the morning we went golfing together, remember that?"

"I remember," I laughed. "But we were knockin' around golf balls, not your balls!"

I found a parking space not far from our court-ordered destination. Once inside, I had a brilliant idea.

"Hey Ted," I said. "There are so many people here, I don't think anyone would know which one of us is which. Why don't I give them my blood?"

"That's why," Ted said, pointing across the room.

And there she was, Miss Hottie State's Attorney, standing with the lab technician.

"Why in the hell," I asked Ted, "would a state's attorney come to the lab for this?"

"Because you pissed her off that day," Ted replied. "And I guess she was smart enough to figure out we'd come together, and maybe try to pull off what you just suggested."

We waited while she continued to speak with the lab tech. I knew Ted was nervous, so I tried to lighten the mood.

"You know what I think, Ted? I think she's going to make you go in one of those little rooms with a bunch of porno and make you whack off!"

"Fuck you, Joey!"

"Oh yeah," I continued. "This woman wants more than blood. She's like a Mrs. Uncle Sam in a recruitment poster. I WANT YOU!"

"Gentlemen," she said, stepping toward us. But this time there were no obligatory hand gestures of politeness, which was fine by us. You never want to get too close to the flame!

"Mr. Polari, you can wait out here," she said.

I could not believe she knew my name. *I must have really, really pissed her off*, I thought to myself. Ted must have told her my name after she had me carried out of the courtroom. I was sure that somewhere I had found eternity in a steno pad filled with accusatory notes.

Well, I thought some more, *she can't make me leave this place, as much as she may want me to.*

"Mr. Grazer, if you'll come with me, the lab technician will draw your blood now."

I watched as they walked off together. Ten minutes later, Ted reappeared in the hallway alone. He looked ashen white.

"Are you okay?" I asked.

"I don't like the sight of blood. And I think they popped my vein," he said, peeling back the bandage and gauze.

"Jesus Christ!" I said, looking at his arm.

"They said I'm okay. I guess they couldn't find a vein."

"Fuck this place," I said. "Let's go have a drink. You look like you need one, anyway."

Ted and I found a bar on Madison Street near the United Center and went inside. It was dark but not foreboding. We pulled out two stools and waited for the bartender to finish his cigarette.

"What'll you guys have?" he asked, blowing smoke in the air as he came toward us.

"Ted," I said, "you go first."

"Yeah, ahh, give us two shots of tequila and I'll have a Dos Equis."

Ted and the bartender looked at me.

"I'll have the same."

Our order arrived and we clanked our shot glasses together. I could feel the tequila hit the back of my throat. I slapped the shot glass down on the bar.

"Burn baby, burn!" I laughed while looking at both of us in the back bar mirror. I reminisced, thinking back to what my father once said to me: "You guys are real characters, aren't you?"

Ted answered that question for me now. "Oh yeah!" he said, slamming the shot glass on the bar upside down.

"I was thinking," I began to say. "When we were at the Daley Center, I was checking out the Picasso in front. You know, it's made of self-weathering Cor-Ten steel, which over time develops a natural rust patina."

"What about it?" Ted asked.

"Well, I think that's what's gonna happen to your penis now," I said, trying to cheer Ted up.

"Probably," Ted said. In seconds he had become very solemn.

"What are you thinking?" I asked.

"I can't believe how bad I've fucked everything up. My wife hates me. My kids hate me. Even the fuckin' dog hates me. A dog, for Christ's sake."

"No one hates you, Ted. Well, maybe a little, but not the dog, I'm sure."

Ted didn't laugh.

"My worthless fuckin' life is over!"

"Look," I said, "Your life is not over. You're barely forty years old. No matter what happens, you'll recover from this and move on."

"You know the restaurant is broke, too. We're going to file bankruptcy."

I was shocked. The restaurant I had built not two years earlier was broke.

"Farah didn't tell me that."

"I didn't think she would," Ted said.

"Is there anything I can do?" I asked.

"Yeah, you can kill me now!"

Not this again, I thought to myself before answering.

"You know, I'd love to take you out of your misery, but I have enough problems."

"I don't know what to do," Ted said as he shrugged his shoulders. "I told her I was sorry, that I know I screwed up, that I was stupid and everything and anything else I could think of. I said we should work it out for the kids' sake if nothing else."

"What'd she say?" I asked, although I already knew the answer.

"She said she wants a divorce and I could take that two-bit whore Jessica and shove her up my ass!"

"She said that?" I asked, although I wasn't shocked by what Farah said.

"She's really pissed, Joey."

"She's hurt, Ted. And she's afraid."

"We talked a little last night. I told her I'd give her everything. The house too, if the bank will let us keep it out of the bankruptcy."

"When did the lab tech say he'd have an answer?" I asked.

"The state's attorney said she'd call me Monday, so I guess that's when."

"Well, let's not sit here until then. I'll take you home. I have to meet Marie this afternoon over at the Merchandise Mart."

"You buyin' stuff for the house?" Ted asked.

"Yeah, but I don't know why I have to go with. Whatever we pick out together, she changes a week later anyway."

"How come women do that?" Ted asked.

"Because they can."

WE DIDN'T TALK MUCH on the way home. I skipped driving the expressway, so we remained westbound on Madison Street. I made a few cracks, no pun intended, about young guys being unable to pull their pants up. Of course, I was riding with a guy who had a similar problem, only more with the zipper portion.

And still, all the alcohol I drank could not stop the sadness I felt for Ted and Farah. I imagined you could forgive a lot of trespasses in a relationship but infidelity was not one of them. I knew I couldn't. I always thought it was one of those basic tenets of marriage that binds two people together. But I guess, as my plumber always said, "Shit happens."

"I'll see you later, man," I said, pulling up in front of Ted's house.

"Yeah, nice day for a blood test, huh?"

"I guess," I replied. "Call me if you need anything."

Monday came soon enough. I always hated Mondays because it gave my customers the entire weekend to think about things to add to their punch list and quest for perfection. Naturally they were all perfect, so they expected me to be. I didn't mind it much, as long as they were willing to pay for it. Thankfully, most of them were.

The phone rang around three-thirty that afternoon. It was Ted. His voice cracked.

"What's the matter?" I asked.

"I never should have told Farah about Jessica."

"Why? What's going on?"

There was a long pause before Ted replied.

"I'm not the father."

"I knew it!" I said.

"But Farah still wants a divorce."

I didn't say it, but I knew that, too.

Roxana Sullivan has been living in Chicago for about three years. She fell in love with the city at first sight, despite its long and cold winters, and that love for the city still continues. In her spare time, Roxana loves taking her dog on long walks through Lincoln Park, enjoying local restaurants, and when she finds the time, writing.

Dead Silent

By Roxana Sullivan

SARAH SAT AT ONE OF THE TABLES outside her favorite wine bar and ordered a glass of rosé. It was early in the afternoon, and she was the only one sitting outside. There were a few people inside the restaurant, but she preferred to sit by herself. She glanced up at the sky and hoped the dark clouds overhead would blow over and that it wouldn't rain.

She didn't want to go in there with all those people. The chatter and occasional laughter from inside ebbed and flowed, but it wasn't inviting in any way. She was alone this afternoon and wanted to keep it that way.

Broadway was a busy street, but sitting out on the sidewalk patio alone did not seem as strange as sitting alone at a bar. Sarah leaned back in her chair and snapped a picture with her phone. She glanced around to see if anybody had noticed her taking the photograph.

Good, she thought. She hated seeing people constantly taking pictures of themselves, their food, their wine or cocktails, their shoes. It was just too much. But the rosé had a beautiful pink color with a slight hue of peach and a radiance to it that made the glass glow against the steely gray sky. *No filter needed for this one,* she thought as she opened her Facebook app.

"Just a quiet afternoon before the rain," she tagged the photo. But she hesitated before posting it.

She hoped that it would get lots of likes. On the other hand, she wasn't sure she wanted people knowing that she was out drinking by herself in the middle of the day. She also didn't want people knowing where she was.

Today was her birthday, but she had no plans. Yesterday afternoon, she had come home from work to find twenty-five of her closest friends crammed into her tiny Lakeview apartment. Her roommate, Joanie, had surprised her with a birthday party. Sarah hated surprises and she hated crowds, but she had smiled when she entered the living room.

She began looking over the pictures from the night before. Joanie had tagged her in all of them, but there were only a couple that Sarah was actually in. The one of her and Joanie had thirty-five likes.

Sarah remembered taking the photo. She had finally worked up the nerve to talk to Nate. Luckily Joanie had remembered to invite him to the party. She walked toward him as he was getting a beer from the fridge and managed to get out a "Hi" – the most she had ever spoken to him. Sarah had often seen him coaching tennis at the East Bank Club, but she had never worked up the nerve to speak to him before.

"I want a picture with the birthday girl!" shouted Joanie. She rushed over, threw her arm around Sarah's shoulder, and put her head close to "the birthday girl's."

"Cute!" Joanie said, examining the selfie. Then she walked away, leaving Sarah alone.

Sarah looked toward the fridge. Nate was gone – already out on the patio talking to a girl someone else had brought along.

Sarah hated parties, especially when they were her parties. She threw dinner parties once or twice a year, but she hated the process. *What if they don't like my food? Did I buy the right wine? Would they want beer instead? Screw what they want, it's my dinner party. What if nobody shows up? What will we talk about? I wonder when they'll leave?*

She wasn't sure why she always put herself through things like this. These parties seemed like a good idea. Most of the time they were Joanie's idea. It was funny, but she always felt most alone when she had other people around. Sarah would go through the motions, listening, smiling, contributing to conversations at just the right time, but inside she felt a quietness and insecurity. *Do these people even like me?*

She admitted that they were better friends online. She seemed to have more conversations with them over text or on social media than she had in person. Her friends seemed so much friendlier on Facebook. There they would ooh and aah at some picture she posted, affirming their friendship through little thumbs-up buttons and showing no sign of disapproval. At the dinner table, there were side glances, nervous laughter, and pauses in conversation. It wasn't just her – everyone seemed as out-of-place having face-to-face conversations as she did, which made the dinner parties even more awkward. And parties, full-on parties…they were even worse.

God! Why don't they just leave?! she had thought an hour into the party. Last night she had really wished that she could have told everyone to head home so she could put on her pajamas, climb into bed and watch reruns of *How I Met Your Mother.* But she bore through it until they were gone – at two-thirty in the morning when the booze finally ran out. She never did get to talk to Nate after that initial "Hi" in the kitchen. And he never came over to talk to her or wish her a happy birthday.

She decided the following morning that she was going to treat herself on her actual birthday. Do what she wanted to do. She got up at eight o'clock that morning, pulled her hair back in a ponytail, and put on her running clothes. She pulled out her phone to check the weather and saw about twenty Facebook posts all wishing her a happy birthday. By the time she returned from her run, there were forty more, including pictures from the night before, and two voicemails from Joanie.

"Hello? Where are you? I got up this morning and waited around for you, but you weren't here. Where did you go? I wanted to see if you wanted to go out for a little birthday brunch and some Bloody Marys. Anna and Veronica want to go, too. Anyway, call me back as soon as you get this."

And then, "Hello? Where are you? You've been gone two hours already. I'm going to meet Anna and Veronica for breakfast. Come join us if you get this in time."

Sarah had stopped by the farmer's market on the way back and had already eaten some breakfast tacos. She was glad she missed those other girls. They were more Joanie's friends than hers.

She made herself a cup of coffee and went to sit out on the balcony so she couldn't hear the phone buzz with new messages and "happy birthday" posts. But she was restless. At any moment Joanie would barge back into their apartment, tell her about brunch, and fill the rest of Sarah's day with plans and agendas.

Sarah hopped in the shower and then put on some clean clothes. It had been much too early to go out to a bar, but she figured she could have a late lunch there, and that would make drinking by herself okay. She just wanted to be out of the house when Joanie returned.

And so she found herself sitting out on the sidewalk patio, not eating, just drinking her wine and hoping the rain would hold off. She felt the first drop on her arm, and then another plopped right in her glass. More drops splattered on the sidewalk around her. Sarah took a couple of gulps of her wine, the acidity hitting the back of her throat like little sharp needles. She left some cash under her glass and quickly hailed a cab.

Sarah didn't know where she wanted to go. She could have just as easily walked home before the rain would fully start coming down.

"Where to?" said the cabbie in a thick Eastern European accent. Ukrainian, Polish, Bulgarian? Sarah always liked to guess. "Lady?" asked the cabbie again.

Sarah felt her phone vibrate. It was Joanie calling again. She hesitated.

"Come on lady. I can't just sit here," said the cabbie.

"Ok. Sorry," responded Sarah looking up from her phone. "1400 S. Lake Shore Drive. The Field Museum, please." She was surprised that she knew the actual address. Her phone kept buzzing and Sarah let the call go to voicemail, placing the phone in her purse. As she and the cabbie made their way down Lake Shore Drive, her phone would periodically buzz. Sometimes it was a single-buzz Facebook post, sometimes a double-buzz text message, and once more a call.

The cab pulled up in front of the magnificent columns and Sarah walked around to the north entrance. She pulled her phone out of her purse to silence it. A Facebook post from a high school friend she hadn't spoken to in years, a missed call from Joanie, and a text message from her as well: "I have someone here who wants to talk to you...PICK UP YOUR PHONE!"

Sarah walked in and bought her ticket. She wandered past Sue the dinosaur and stared up at its toothy grin. Her phone rang in her hand. She looked down to see who it was. It was Nate. "That's who Joanie must have been talking about," she thought. "Are they hanging out right now?" The phone rang and she wondered if she should answer. *What would I say? Why was he calling? Why didn't he just talk to her at the party last night?* Sarah stared at Nate's name on the screen, her finger hovering over the green Accept button. A child running by bumped into her, and she glanced up.

ANCIENT EGYPT, the sign in front of her said. The phone rang again. It was Nate again. She was going to answer this time. Sarah stepped down the stone staircase into the three-story tomb as she glanced down at her phone, her finger hitting the Accept button.

"Hello?" she answered. "Hello?"

There was no response. "Nate? Joanie? Is this some sort of joke?"

No answer.

Now, deep inside the tomb, she looked down at her phone and realized she had lost reception.

Rose McInerney is a social justice advocate and philanthropist, utilizing her strategic management and teaching background to manage a family foundation in support of youth mentorship. Rose also spends time writing and photo journaling her travels abroad, highlighting stories about cultural diversity and women. All other time is spent watching movies, reading, drinking wine, and enjoying the company of family, friends, and her two dogs.

Night Snow

By Rose McInerney

SHE'S PREGNANT. Ernesto carried this thought and an overwhelming feeling of betrayal into the hallway of his fiftieth-floor condo. His fingers tapped at the sides of his overcoat as he waited for the elevator door to open. Once inside the sleek, mirrored interior, he rode alone to the ground floor.

Glancing at his reflection, he leaned forward to pick out a small red pepper flake caught in his teeth before rubbing his hands over his face. The pressure of his fingers felt good as they pushed the tension from under the small folds of his tanned skin and the years of resolve that seemed to have suddenly aged him. Ernesto lifted his coat sleeve to check his watch before pulling at his shirt collar. A tiny glint of light sparkled from his polished silver and black onyx cufflink.

He had been late getting home but expected Silvia to be ready. Instead, she was dressed in jeans and sitting on their living room couch.

"I'm pregnant, Ernie," she said as he walked through the door.

Ernesto stopped moving.

"I know," she added.

"I don't know what to say, Sil." Both were silent until Silvia spoke.

"Really?" She paused for a long moment before standing up and lifting her arms from her sides. "Is that it?" she added, raising her voice loud enough for the neighbors to hear. Ernesto moved toward her but she headed toward their bedroom down the hall. He called after her, hoping to diffuse the situation,

"Let's go to the party, Silvia. We'll talk later… when… you know, when we've had time to consider everything."

"After the party? Really, Ernie? Silvia replied, not breaking her step. "It's always *after* with you, isn't it, Ernesto? How about now?" she said, suddenly turning to face him before sitting down on the edge of the bed.

Ernesto saw her eyes welling up but looked away, quickly escaping into the closet. "I'm going to change my shirt. I'll be a minute."

"Take *all* the time you need Ernie," Silvia said emphatically. "What's the rush." But she continued talking anyway as Ernesto let the words slide among the wrinkle-free shirts that lined his closet. Grabbing a shirt from the hanger, Ernesto lingered in its smooth texture before reappearing.

By the time he did, Silvia had stopped talking. Her body looked like it had folded into itself as she aimed her dry, swollen eyes at him, before whispering, "I can't wait, Ernie. It's not just about you anymore." After a moment, she added, "I may not be here when you get back."

Words failed Ernesto. He wanted to tell Silvia she deserved more, but he couldn't. He had to go for a few short hours, and the cold winter air would clear his head and the confusion he felt over what to do about this unplanned twist in their seven-year relationship. As the elevator landed on the ground floor, Ernesto stepped into the shiny, marble lobby. He walked past the vaulted floor-to-ceiling windows, rounding the corner toward the concierge desk. With each step, as his black patent-leather Prada shoes clicked, he felt a renewed sense of rhythm until – *smash*.

Mrs. Dilber, one of Ernesto's neighbors, was coming from the mailroom and slammed into him. Reeling backwards, she landed on her buttocks, and the bundle of mail she had been carrying scattered across the floor.

"Ugh…." she yelped, her legs splaying out from underneath her.

Ernesto stared down at a stunned Mrs. Dilber. Her giant, bulbous eyes fluttered for a few seconds, eclipsing the other tiny features of her face. But Ernesto snapped into form, horrified by the mishap but avoiding eye contact with her as he gushed, "I'm so sorry, Mrs. Dilber. Please let me help you up."

"Well, er, … thanks, Ernesto. That was quite a wallop," she said, grabbing for his extended hand. She smoothed her sweater and forced a chuckle, saying, "If I didn't know better I'd think you were looking for a fight."

Ernesto ignored her chatter as he pulled her dwarfed five-foot frame upright and gathered the letters and grocery flyers on the floor.

"As long as you're okay, Mrs. Dilber." With a quick nod, he turned to leave, but Mrs. Dilber stepped in front, catching his coat sleeve.

"What's wrong, Ernesto? Are you okay?"

"Bah. Um," he muttered pulling his arm away. "I'm fine."

Mrs. Dilber called after him as he hurried off, "Nice bumping into you, anyway. Tell Silvia I'm finished with the book she loaned me. I was hoping to give her…"

Ernesto raced away. *Who does she thinks she is? Always asking questions and pulling Silvia and me into her world – putting her nose in our relationship and things that are none of her business!* Ernesto wished Silvia could be more private like he was; she had shared too much with Mrs. Dilber about his father leaving, her family history, and his job with SkyLab Pharmaceuticals. Thank God he had never told Silvia about his abusive father or his miserable childhood.

Ernesto pulled on his leather gloves and tucked his chin inside his cashmere coat as he raced past James, the doorman, who shouted after him, "Evening, Mr. Cosegro. Bundle up – the snowstorm is coming in a little earlier than expected."

THE WINTER NIGHT AIR WAS BELOW FREEZING, and it slapped Ernesto's lungs as he stepped into it. The wind howled and twisted his deep, chestnut-colored hair, pulling it up by the scalp. Something strange hovered in the air and the haunting moon overhead, but Ernesto was immune to it. He was determined to get to the party, and he'd figure out what to say to Silvia when he returned. Gentle, mesmerizing white snowflakes danced around him in the orchestrated night air. The wind teased the tail of his plaid scarf like a noose.

Outside his building, there was a vortex of wind from the surrounding skyscrapers. Tonight it was particularly strong, making it difficult for Ernesto to walk to the corner of Columbus Avenue and Randolph Street, where he planned to hail a cab. When the wind suddenly changed course, throwing him forward and then back again, he lost his balance and almost slipped to the ground before crying out, "God damn it."

Rushing along Randolph Street, Ernesto noticed a blue haze from the BlueCross BlueShield sign that hung over the street corner. It cast an eerie shadow in the mix of snow, whose intensity had seemed to increase just in the last few minutes. Passing by a rusted metal staircase, Ernesto felt a warm waft of air from the desolate street below. Chicago was full of old stairways that connected upper and lower level streets, and the temperatures down below were always noticeably warmer. Here, the air was sheltered and heated by the frequent trucks and vans that used the city's underbelly as a traffic shortcut from the bustling street life above.

Passing through the ghostly streaks of blue snow, Ernesto glanced down before a low guttural voice interrupted his thoughts: "Help me out mister?" A dark-cloaked figure thrust out a shivering, thick hand. The deep, foreboding voice behind the strong chin and still, calm eyes caught Ernesto off guard. The figure's clean white teeth, the kind not lacking for dental care or suffering from the effects of drug addiction, flashed in the dark as Ernesto's eyes shifted quickly to the beggar's outstretched hand.

Ernesto burrowed his hands in his pockets, giving the stranger hope until he saw Ernesto's vacant eyes narrow and his chin tuck into his coat. The voice gently closed his empty hand as Ernesto yelled, "Taxi."

THE CAB SPED OFF, PULLING UP A FEW MINUTES LATER in front of the Sheraton Hotel, where Ernesto hurried up the escalator to join the party in the ballroom. It was filled with SkyLab employees and their partners, all reveling in the holiday celebration. Tiny reflective, multicolored lights from the Swarovski crystal chandelier hanging overhead danced around them and the small bistro tables that were draped in festive gold tulle.

Ernesto headed for the far corner bar and ordered a whiskey straight. The drink warmed his throat as he surveyed the party and various stations of people. Everyone looked happy; they were talking, laughing, and mingling with ease.

Ernesto felt a slight pang but continued to move about the room until George Shay shouted out to him, "Hey Monsieur!"

"Good evening, George. Good to see you," Ernesto replied. He noticed that his boss's tie was slightly crooked. Gloria, George's current wife, was usually glued to his side but was nowhere in sight.

George slurred back at Ernesto, "You too. Where's that beautiful Silvia?"

"She's not feeling well. Where's your Gloria?" Ernesto chirped.

George was short and squat, and he looked like a penguin with his tuxedo black wings and flipper pants that clung to his white, puffy chest. "Oh, she's around. She's socializing and getting another drink, I'm sure. Shame about Silvia – I like that girl, Ernie."

I'm sure you do, Ernesto thought, having seen George fawn over her in the past. "Yes, she's great." Ernesto said. *Why is George suddenly calling me Ernie? Only Silvia calls me Ernie.*

"Any plans to tie the knot, Ernie?" George baited.

"We'll see, George. I'm not sure, but I actually wanted to talk to you about something. You know that recent merger deal? Well, I didn't get a chance to tell you that I've been thinking..."

"What's with the work shit, Ernie? It's time to relax, take in the season, if you know what I mean. But you're probably pretty happy in that department, I suppose," George added with a slight wink. "Let's talk hockey – how about those Blackhawks?"

"Yes indeed, we're headed for the Cup this year," Marty piped in. He walked into the conversation with George and Ernesto, giving George a friendly slap on the back. Marty was the company head of marketing, and his latest girlfriend Sherri had attended the office picnic this past summer. She was tugging at Marty's sleeve despite his best effort to ignore her.

Ernesto watched as Marty pulled his arm away and motioned behind George's body for Sherri to leave him alone. Seeing his refusal, she thrust herself forward, chest first. Her black dress was cut low and barely covered her voluptuous breasts.

"Pleasure to see you, Ernesto and George," she grinned.

"Hi, Sherri. You look lovely," George said, smiling back at her invitation to look. Ernesto nodded politely, noticing Sherri's smeared lipstick and thick eye makeup. He was embarrassed for Marty and thankful for Silva's humility and grace.

"Well, thank you. You're always a gentleman, Georgy. Marty was just going to get me a drink, weren't you, sweetie?"

Sherri wobbled as she gestured to Marty, who caught her by the waist as she stumbled.

"No tickling, Marty," she giggled, swatting at him but hitting George on the shoulder and teetering onto his foot.

George's hands reached for her, and Ernesto thought he saw George sniff her hair.

Marty squeezed her and responded, "I'll head to the bar in a minute, honey. Maybe you want to visit the ladies' room first, dear."

Marty whispered something in Sherri's ear and George chimed in, "Sounds like a plan, Sherri. I don't know what's happened to Gloria. Its always a pleasure," George said, looking past her to another group of ladies by the buffet table. "And Ernie," he said winking at him, "let's talk tomorrow. Tell Silvia I hope she's better soon. A little advice: skip the talking head stuff tonight and enjoy yourself."

Ernesto stood alone and off to the side of the room, wishing he could have talked more with George. He spent the next half hour gulping whiskey and thinking about Silvia. He didn't know what to make of George's comments. This was the first party she had missed, and he felt rattled. He didn't feel like networking with the other division heads anymore.

Several drinks later, Ernesto headed home. It felt warmer outside, so he passed the cabs lined up outside the hotel entrance. He knew he needed to sober up and decide what he should say to Silvia. Before now, he hadn't really thought about whether or not she meant what she said. It dawned on him, *What if she isn't there when I get back?*

Ernesto decided he should walk a little faster as he rounded the corner of Shula's Steak House and crossed the cobblestone bridge over the Chicago River. He was on the middle level of the city roadway and would have to walk up a few flights of stairs at Wacker Drive to get to the upper level of Columbus Drive, before heading over to Randolph Street. Ernesto looked down at the numbers on his chronometric precision Rolex: Eleven-ten p.m. He could be home by eleven-twenty-five, if he didn't slow.

The city seemed peaceful. *So she was pregnant? We could work this out together and decide what to do. Why would I ever think she did this on purpose?* Now the snow was falling from the sky in giant fluffy flakes, dotting the white shoreline and deepening the blackness of the river below. The moon's reflection in the water created a path of light, joining the river to the large still body of Lake Michigan. He felt alive going home to Silvia.

What he failed to notice were the two dark-hooded men who had followed him from the hotel. The taller one pulled out his cell phone twenty yards from the corner from where Ernesto was headed. Hitting the keypad, he typed, "Cd b 1 (space) 1 min. (space) wait up top 4 him."

Ernesto pictured climbing into bed with Silvia and nestling his warm body against hers. In her anger she would pretend not to notice him, but he would wrap his arms around her still-slim waist like he always did and listen to the rise and fall of her breathing. When he pictured her tear-streaked face, he knew he was wrong to leave her. As Ernesto gripped the handrail and began his ascent, the metal echo of shoes on the stairway above hurried closer.

A sudden blow hit Ernesto in the chest. It was followed by a loud crunch that vibrated through him. He struggled to breathe, looking up wildly and trying to focus on the dark figure whose outstretched leg hovered above him. A heavy work boot obscured his perpetrator's face and lingered in the air during the second before Ernesto realized he was hopelessly falling away from it.

His arms flailed out to the side, desperately hoping to catch the handrail and stop his terrifying descent.

He twisted sideways, futilely missing the rail while hearing a muffled voice: "Goin' somewhere?" One, two, four, and six steps... he rolled to the base of the staircase, writhing in pain.

Another dark figure joined in the assault as Ernesto let out a horrifying scream. His body was thrown down another flight of stairs, tumbling over itself, as his neck snapped backwards and his arms smashed against the side rails. The staircase shook with a steely groan under the continued assault, and Ernesto was powerless against the dark forces.

Ernesto sensed he was in grave danger and struggled to get up, but he felt his entire body throb as the taste of putrid bile mixed with blood filled his throat and spewed onto the hard pavement. He felt a thick stickiness on his hands as he lifted them up to his head in an attempt to stop the loud drumming noise.

The rush of feet converging on him, the assailant from above and the two men who had followed him from the hotel added to the panic that the assault was not over.

As a small crimson streak of blood pooled around Ernesto's head and he fought to stay conscious, Ernesto heard himself moan, "What do you... who...?" But the two remaining slits of light began to fade, eclipsed by the dark shadows that stood above him.

"Get his money, you dumb f***... hurry up...he's f***** bleeding," the first voice said.

Another voice sounded more desperate. "Let's get outta here or we'll hafta beat him to death."

"Not 'til we get what we came for!" the first voice said, rummaging through Ernesto's pockets and stripping him of his wallet and watch.

"What if he saw us…maybe we gotta do him," a new and more nervous voice interrupted. Ernesto fought to stay awake. He heard a clicking sound like something opening, and a glint of steel wavered above him in the moonlight. He couldn't understand what the figures were saying. He felt himself drifting away from his body, but something sharp pulled him back, refusing to let him go. It was Silvia. He saw her face and a thousand tiny, warm pricks from the tears running down her face pierced him. *I'm going to die,* he thought, *and Silvia will be alone having our baby. I can't leave her.*

He worried only for her now as he slipped further from his paralyzed body and into a white sea of forgiveness. A calm washed over him as he realized for the first time that he loved Silvia. He loved her more than life itself. The secrets he had kept from the world were lifted from his heavy heart. He embraced the forgiveness that came from the depths of his despair and the knowledge of Silvia's gift.

Oblivious to the rapid succession of kicks that continued to shake his back and legs, Ernesto heard a piercing battle cry before he blacked out. The shrieking scream came from the feverish eyes of a stranger who had heard the clanking metal sounds on the stairway and Ernesto's cry for help. The hero was a veteran soldier with powerful hands and a fearless heart, the kind that comes from years of military training and witnessing the horrors of war up close.

The soldier had watched men blown from Humvee vehicles in Iraq only to return home a stranger in his own country. Living on the streets, he protected himself and others with his own sense of social justice. The criminals who had attacked Ernesto had violated his rules and threatened control over his turf. They realized quickly that they were no match for his brute strength and brazen vehemence. In one swoop, the soldier had knocked the attacker's knife free with the mighty swing of a discarded gunmetal curtain rod that he had fashioned into a bayonet. Several debilitating blows to the head and body convinced them to retreat, allowing the soldier to carry Ernesto to safety.

ERNESTO'S EYELIDS SPUTTERED OPEN several hours later on Lower Wacker Drive just in from the corner of Water Street. His nostrils twitched from the stench of nearby rotting garbage, and the stagnant air and absence of any audible city noises unnerved him. Reaching down to the source of an uncomfortable throbbing pain in his right arm, Ernesto wondered what had happened and who had wrapped the tight, bloodstained bandage cradling his arm.

Straining to see against the balls of light under the heavy steel beams overhead, Ernesto saw a small group of homeless men gathered near by. They lay huddled in what appeared to be a mini-shantytown of broken cardboard boxes lined up in a zigzag pattern across the sidewalk. There was no room for anyone to pass by the broken hovels butted up against the cracked, concrete walls.

Ernesto tried to speak, "Ugh… what… where the… hell?"

A clear, calm voice rang out in response, "Shut up."

A thick forearm hit Ernesto's right arm, stressing the seriousness of the message. Ernesto winced in pain and twisted his head sideways in search of the commanding voice.

"Don't move, either. You'll make it worse," the voice added.

None of this made any sense to Ernesto.

"Take this," the voice demanded again.

Tapping a smooth bottle filled with a smelly liquid and pressing it against Ernesto's lips, the stranger spilled the liquid into his mouth. A burning sensation slid down his throat, bringing relief.

"Who are you?" Ernesto stammered.

Black and gray dots clouded his vision as he raised his left arm to the crown of his head, discovering a crusty, clumped mass that gave way to a still waxy spot underneath. This triggered his memory – the beating flashed through his mind.

"Oh, God - no!" he said.

Ernesto spastically flung his left arm underneath him, expecting it to support his weight. But he was too weak, and his face hit the concrete pavement.

"Shit!"

This brought the attention of a new voice voice, accompanied by the sound of a rolling empty glass. "Waz going on there Bo?" the voice called out.

Silence.

The new voice didn't wait long.

"I'm gonna piss on ya head for takin' tha betta houzz box and hoggin the juice, Bo."

Ernesto wondered, *what kind of a name is Bo?*

Then came the sound of the flimsy partition being pushed back against the wall and a shuffling sound, as the stranger came toward Ernesto.

The voice belonging to Bo answered quickly,

"Easy, Slater. I told you there was nothin' ta see here. Got another friend for the night. That's all. I'm not holding out on you… just coming in a second to give you and Taz the rest of the juice."

"Ya betta, Bo. I know you're a pal, Bo, but whatcha goin' and bringin' another body down here for? Whaz he contri-butin'?"

Slater, a tall, slender man with dirty blonde hair poking out from a skullcap, stumbled into view. He was close enough that Ernesto could see his face. It looked like Slater's teeth had rotted from years of drug abuse, and Ernesto felt a wave of nausea as Slater moved toward him.

I'll close my eyes for just a few seconds and then I'll get up.

But he couldn't. Ernesto lay helplessly littered across the payment, blending in with the homeless men. His clothes were tattered and his pockets turned inside out. Attempting to lift himself up, Ernesto turned to get a better look at the small crowd that had started to gather. Another tall figure stood out. He was stockier than Slater and walked with a limp. A gruff, raspy voice yelled out.

"He'll hafta get the hell outta here, Bo. He's a devil, Bo. Look at him, Bo. Devil, devil, devil. Nothin' but trouble." Yanking on his ears and rubbing his face, the deep voice continued, shaking a condemning finger at Ernesto, "Can't ya see he's bad? He's bad, Bo. Look at 'im. He's one of them, Bo. Bad, bad, bad."

"Easy, Taz. Go back and lie down. I'm taking care of business tonight. Remember… it's my watch and I say what goes. He's nobody. There's no war tonight."

But Taz wasn't convinced, and he and Slater started arguing about what to do.

"He's goin' ta bring trouble. I knows it." Taz starting shaking his fists and swearing with increased ferocity, revving up Slater. Ernesto wondered what second calamity was about to befall him just as flashing blue lights bounced off the concrete walls.

A police car pulled up beside them, and the officer on the passenger side yelled out, "Evening, boys. Everything okay here?"

Bo jumped in front of the ruckus to respond, "Hey'a Rick. Ya – all good. Taz and Slater are jus' havin' a little political discussion, but it's cool. How's it going?"

"Slow night," the officer responded, leaning out his car window. His partner was busy talking to someone on the phone. "The mayor's office is talking about moving you guys from this section too, Bo. Just keep the guys quiet but you might be looking for a new spot soon. Do you need anything?"

"Don't they know those hostels ain't safe, Rick? Taz and Slater are safer with me, and we're running outta places to go. I won't go back there."

"I know, Bo. Don't mean to get you going. I'm just letting you know the word on the street."

"Thanks, Rick," Bo said. "I appreciate that, and I actually do need something. You see, there's this guy here you gotta help." Bo turned toward Ernesto, stepping away from the car.

The officer looked over to see what Bo was talking about, when a dispatch voice rang out.

Bo bent down to lift Ernesto into the car but Rick yelled out, "Sorry, Bo. Gotta run.

10-15 in progress…some guy threatening his wife."

"But Rick, I gotta guy here," Bo said, carrying Ernesto toward the cruiser.

Ernesto heard the car screech away, the siren drowning out any hope of his rescue. He yelped as Bo placed him back down on the payment, knocking his injured arm. The sling had not stopped the swelling in Ernesto's arm but it had helped to restrict its movement. Leaning against the concrete wall along the sidewalk, Ernesto watched Taz and Slater rummage through Bo's blankets looking for some of the drink he had promised.

Slater shot out, "I can't see the juice, Bo. Where's the damn juice ya promised?"

"It's there, Slater. Give me a sec," Bo said as he pointed toward the ground, where a bent piece of rusted metal railing was ripped from the concrete walkway. Beside it was a bottle of whiskey wrapped in a crumpled brown bag.

It suddenly occurred to Ernesto that he had missed an opportunity. "Was that a siren I heard?"

"Yep. Sorry, but you'll have to wait," Bo said, raising his hand. Taz threw his fists up at Bo and started yelling, "I ain't goin' ta wait Bo!"

"No, no. Not you Taz. I'm talking to the guy lying here." Bo said, grabbing the whisky that Taz and Slater wanted. "Here ya go. As for you," he said, looking down at Ernesto, "I got another plan to get you outta here."

"A plan?" Ernesto said cautiously, trying again to hold himself up on his good side.

"What'd you say your name was?" Bo asked

"I didn't. It's Ernesto. Ernesto Cosegro."

"Ok Cosegro. I'll call you Cuz. I've seen enough of you tonight to forgive the scrooge attitude." Ernesto frowned as Bo continued, "Don't worry, Frank will circle 'round soon. He'll give you a ride. I can't carry you back up all those stairs to the upper street level now; I need to stay here for the other guys."

Ernesto didn't understand. *What did Bo mean by calling me Cuz and who was Frank? What did he mean, watching over the guys?* His side began to cramp with pain, but Ernesto focused on Bo's face. "Why did you help me out tonight when those punks beat me up? Do I know you?"

Bo stared back, so Ernesto pushed him further, saying, "Who are you?"

Smiling broadly, Bo flashed his pearly white teeth at Ernesto and watched his eyes widen and the remaining color drain from his skin. Bo grinned, "That's right, Cuz. Now you know me, don't you?"

"Oh, God. You're the guy I walked past tonight, aren't you? But…I didn't help you." Ernesto stuttered.

"Whatever," Bo said. "Guys like us are invisible. To you people we're all the same."

"That's not true," Ernesto said, as his heart raced to the truth. "No. You're absolutely right."

Ernesto reluctantly welcomed the smile on Bo's face and started to apologize, saying, "I wish I had..." before his confession was abruptly cut off by a mechanical swooshing sound and a powerful shot of air. It was the sound of brakes coming to a full stop in front of a cluster of cardboard boxes. Ernesto saw the puffy outline of a man hanging onto the back of the city's sky-blue recycling vehicle with the words CONSERVE CHICAGO TOGETHER written in bold lettering. Bo swaggered over to meet the man.

"Hey, Frank. I got someone I want you to meet," Bo said.

MEANWHILE, BACK AT THE CONDO, Silvia awoke to the sounds of the early morning traffic and the sun streaming in through the blinds left up. When the phone rang she hurried to the elevator.

Luis had started his shift on the front desk and rushed to meet Ernesto as he limped into the lobby, held up by the big burly man wearing a city worker uniform and a winter jacket marked with a neon reflective X on his back.

"What in God's name happened, Mr. Cosegro?" Luis exclaimed, rushing over and grabbing Ernesto's waist.

"I'm okay, Luis, but you need to call Silvia." Frank and Luis helped him stagger to the couch as Luis said, "I'm calling an ambulance, sir."

"Is she still here, Luis?"

"Don't know, sir, but I'll call her right after I call for help," Luis said, offering for Ernesto to lean on him as he helped him sit on the lobby couch. A minute later, he called over to Ernesto, "Ambulance is coming. and she's on her way down too. Hold tight, Mr. Cosegro."

"Thank God," Ernesto said, grimacing in pain as he looked out the window. "I don't how to thank you, Frank. You were so good to help me, and Bo, well...I don't know if I'll ever be..."

"Think nothing of it," Frank interrupted. "Just take care and I'm glad to help. Bo could use some too, you know. That would be something. Maybe he'd listen to you."

"Thanks, Frank. I won't forget it. Tell Bo I'll be around in a day or so. We've got some talking to do," Ernesto said, starting to feel light-headed but motioning with his chin for Frank to get going.

Looking out the window, Ernesto took a deep breath and stared at the layer of snow covering the garden. He considered the storm that had raged overnight and his last words to Silvia before leaving. He embraced the strange and mixed feelings of excitement and nervousness that pushed through his queasiness. The faint sound of sirens could be heard approaching, but he turned to look for Silvia at the exact moment she walked into the lobby.

"Oh my God! What happened, Ernie?" she said when she saw his bloodied head and bandaged arm strapped against his torn, dirtied shirt.

"I'm sorry, Silvia. I've been sick thinking about you. Can you forgive me?" he said softly.

"Are you hurt? You're a mess – what happened?"

Ernesto's future rested in Silvia's frightened face. It was here and now and he wanted it more than anything he had ever wanted. Ernesto put his left hand on Silvia's stomach as she stared back at him in confusion. Before he could answer, Luis was ushering in the ambulance crew that had arrived.

Lifting his hand and sliding it down by Silvia's side, Ernesto linked his palm in hers saying, "I've been a fool, Silvia – I love you."

Silvia hesitated as Ernesto added, "Will you come with me?"

Karen Ebert Yancey is a writer and conservationist who grew up along the Lake Michigan shore. A former newspaper reporter, her poetry has appeared in more than a dozen regional and national publications. She is a co-editor and writer for the nonfiction book, The Nature of Door.

The Man Without A Wake

By Karen Ebert Yancey

ERIC WAS 24 YEARS OLD WHEN HE LEARNED of Frank's death. He was walking north over the Michigan Avenue bridge still awestruck at the good fortune that had landed him a job at one of the largest advertising agencies in the city during a major recession. The alabaster tower of the Wrigley Building gleamed in the midday light, and he was so full of the joy of life before that moment that he seemed to bounce across the bridge. The Chicago River, usually green and flat, shimmered in the sunlight as the first spring kayakers paddled toward the lake. His new suit fit his athletic build like a glove; he smiled as two young women in high heels and light khaki coats eyed him as he approached.

Shorter, red-haired Henry walked beside him, another new recruit. They were returning from a client meeting further south on the avenue; they had been accompanied by one of the vice presidents from the firm who had to rush out to another meeting.

"Hard to believe that old man Frank is no longer with us," Henry said.

"What do you mean?" said Eric. "Are you talking about Frank Schmitz, the guy in the creative department? He really helped me out with a good slogan I needed for that appliance company last month."

"He died, Eric…two days ago," said Henry. "Didn't you get the email?"

"No, man, unless I erased it by accident," said Eric.

"Some disease, like Lou Gehrig's, but it came on real suddenly," said Henry.

Eric thought of Frank, his ruddy face, kind smile and the way he called him "kid." Why, he had asked Frank a question, something about where to find a thesaurus, just two weeks ago and Frank had led him back to the small, dusty closet where they kept old books with information that sometimes still couldn't be found with a Google search.

"Well, when is the funeral?" said Eric. "I should go."

"No, nothing," said Henry. "His wife decided not to do anything."

"I never heard of that," said Eric. They were passing the glittering shop windows and were heading back to their offices. Eric thought how sad it was that Frank had died without ever getting one of the corner offices overlooking Lake Shore Drive and Michigan Avenue. They were reserved for the senior ad executives. What had his title been again? Advertising manager, he thought.

Eric shook his thick curly hair as if trying to rid it of flies. He closed his eyes and pictured his Irish Catholic grandfather's funeral with all the cars lined up at Holy Name Cathedral. It had been a cold Chicago fall day, the raindrops like spears hitting his face as he held the umbrella, trying to shield his mother and sister as they hurried from the car to the church. They stumbled and lurched in their heels up the stairs to the cathedral, his mother holding her large hat down to prevent it from blowing away. The church was already half full when they arrived, the intimidating altar garish and magnificently adorned with flowers from his grandfather's many friends and business associates. He had ushered his mother and sister to the front pew where a long line of his uncles, aunts, and cousins already sat. His father, his hair flattened by his run through the rain, squeezed into the end of the pew a few minutes later. There was a full choir singing "Ave Maria" as six of his cousins carried his grandfather's marble casket, heaped with white roses, down the long red-carpeted aisle. The stone pillars of the cathedral seemed to shake with the sheer power of the music. His mother and sister wept, and the music even brought tears to his father's eyes when Eric stole a glance. Eric, himself, had to use all his male powers to stifle a cry of anguish.

When the casket was laid at the front of the church, a soloist sang "A Mighty Fortress Is Our God," seeming to express all the agony of death. But the priest preached redemption and celebration of his grandfather's life.

Eric had liked that. How he had revered his grandfather, one of seven brothers, who had worked his way through Loyola's Law School and built a law practice and a family of five children with Eric's grandmother, Colleen. He remembered the big Christmas celebrations at his grandparents' house, the floor awash in wrapping paper and the room a bedlam of more than twenty grandchildren playing with the new toys his grandfather, dressed as Santa Claus, had handed each child from his red bag. There had been the special tent for the O'Malley family at the St. Patrick's Day parade each year, his grandfather always by the bar, proudly handing out green beer to any adult friend that stopped by.

"There are so many lives that this man touched," the priest had exclaimed in his eulogy. And Eric had heard those around him weeping for the loss of his grandfather. His grandmother sat crying softly in front, two of his aunts on either side to comfort her. He had almost expected to see his grandfather, his white, cropped hair, sitting beside her as he had done at every Sunday mass in the cathedral for more than fifty years.

Since that day more than a year ago, Eric had tried to reconcile this image with other facts he had learned about his grandfather from his older brother, Mark. His grandfather had been part of the Grayland investigation in Chicago, a group of attorneys tried and convicted for bribing judges to keep murderers they were representing for the Italian Mafia out of jail.

"It wasn't like grandpa was letting dangerous criminals out on the street," Mark had explained. "The Mafia's hit men only killed other criminals, not innocent bystanders."

"But grandpa took that dirty money to pay the judges off and pocketed some himself," Eric had reminded Mark. "I bet that was the money he used to take us all to Disney World one Easter. The time the O'Malleys all formed a line behind Mickey Mouse and led the parade at the park."

"Jeez, Eric, I don't know. What does it matter?" Mark had become irritated with him then and stopped the discussion. "Grandpa was out of jail years before you were born, so I doubt it was that money that he squirreled away for Disney. He did his time in jail."

Mark was an attorney in the family firm himself, which in spite of the indictments, had grown and thrived in the last decades and continued its close ties with the Italians. "You can always trust an Irish lawyer to do the right thing by us," said Anthony Verito, one of the Mafia's more well-known leaders. It was an endorsement that made Mark proud.

That was one of the reasons Eric had steered away from law school. He didn't want to be cornered into making those choices.

And then there was Frank, who never hurt a flea, a truly nice person who went through the world helping everybody out. "I guess he didn't have a family then," said Eric to Henry as they rode in the elevator back to their tenth-floor offices.

"No kids, anyway," said Henry. "Well, I got to get back to work on the Abcock campaign."

Eric had work to do, too. As he headed to his cubicle of an office, one step up from the intern desks in the middle of the work area, he couldn't get Frank out of his mind, and he had a big campaign for the Hilton Hotels due next week.

Finally, after an hour of staring at his computer screen, he got up and walked over to get some coffee, stopping by Henry's office.

"Couldn't find that email about Frank in my inbox," he said to Henry, who was typing furiously. "Could you forward it to me when you have a minute?"

"Yea, right," said Henry, not even looking up from his screen.

About an hour later, it showed up in his inbox and Eric immediately opened it. It was from their office manager, Kyle Lang:

I regret to inform you that Frank Schmitz, an employee of Leo Bates Co. for the last 20 years, passed away quietly yesterday after a short illness. Frank joined the company in 1994 and worked diligently on a variety of accounts. He was a dedicated employee. Frank is survived by his wife, Irene. No services are planned. He will be missed by all of us at Leo Bates.

Eric thought again about his grandfather. There were so many grandchildren that Eric couldn't remember his grandfather ever spending a minute of time with him alone. As he grew older, his grandfather always turned to one of his sons and said, "Whose child is this again?" He had trouble remembering his grandchildren's names even before his fast decline from throat cancer at eighty-five.

He thought of plain-looking Frank, who greeted everyone in the firm by their name and remembered whose child was sick and who had a birthday. Frank was only sixty. His most distinguishing feature had been his rich, booming voice – he had told Eric he had once been a radio announcer. Like many novices, shortly after they had joined the firm last fall, Eric and Henry had waited too long to put together a PowerPoint presentation of a campaign for a dot-com company, and it had been Frank who had stayed at the office with them until midnight and helped them pull it all together. "You're going to be brilliant at tomorrow's meeting," he had told them, then stepped back and let them take all the credit when they won the account.

Wasn't anyone going to do anything about Frank? he wondered all day.

The next day in a staff meeting on the Hilton account, Eric waited to bring up Frank until the end of the meeting. "Pretty sad about Frank Schmitz," he said to the table of young account executives all dressed in their best dark attire.

"Yeah, I heard about that," said Erin, chewing on her gum. "Who would have thought he would go so fast."

"Tough break," said Henry, who was part of the meeting. "Don't know that there is much that we can do. Leo Bates always sends a plant at times like that."

"A plant?" said Eric, trying to hide his irritation. "That's all they send to the family after twenty years of service?"

"Relax, Eric," said Henry. "I agree that Frank was a nice guy. What more do you want us to do? His wife said they weren't religious and there wasn't any other family."

"I don't know," said Eric. "It seems a guy's life should count for more than a plant."

"That's really up to the family," said Erin, still smacking her gum.

IT WAS A BEAUTIFUL SPRING NIGHT, so Eric decided to walk home after work to the Wellington Avenue apartment he shared with two of his former college roommates. They had called him earlier to meet at Butch McGuire's, but he told them he wasn't into it.

"Tough day at work. I'm going go home and watch TV," he told them.

He stretched his walk out along the lakeshore path and took another detour out onto the North Avenue pier. His hands were in his pockets as he eyed the handsome figure he made in the reflection of the glass kiosks that advertised summer events along the lakefront.

The ice had melted and the water looked blue and clear in the fading daylight. Lake Michigan had always been the ever-present backdrop to his life, growing up in the city. He wanted to start emailing his friends to mark the dates for the best Northerly Island concerts of the summer. He sat down for a minute at the end of the pier, carefully wiping off the cement to keep the pants of his new suit clean. His new loafers dangled near the water; the waves lapped gently at the pylons below him.

Still, he couldn't get Frank out of his head. Was it because some people who had a checkered life like his grandfather died with the funeral drama of an important man, while people who were good and quietly helpful like Frank left the earth without a whimper? No mourning, no wake, no funeral.

"Straight to the cremator; ashes to ashes and dust to dust," he mumbled at the lake.

How could life be so crazy? How could death be so unfair? Eric had been thinking of himself as a big shot, landing a job at a top ad agency right out of college. Now, he saw that his life could end up just like Frank's, without ever achieving a corner office, a place in the history of Leo Bates.

In fact, there might not even be a Leo Bates Advertising Agency in twenty years. In this age of corporate mergers, it could easily be taken over by another firm. Even the stories of the firm's great leaders would eventually be wiped off a computer disk, relegated to a basement file somewhere.

Usually the lake soothed him. He watched a seagull soaring on currents of wind as the evening light illuminated the lake. Tonight, however, he felt so deflated . . . and angry. Here at twenty-four, he thought he finally understood life, had gotten a hold of a good thing with his job. Next, there would be a wife. Maybe kids, maybe not. It had all seemed so important. He had felt so important.

And he wasn't. Perhaps that had been Frank's final act of goodness – to humble him.

"If there is a heaven, you deserve to be up there, buddy," he said to the lake and the sky. A couple, standing a few feet away, eyed him warily.

He stood up and retreated from the pier. No one noticed that he walked less jauntily than before, his shoulders slightly stooped.

Bill Trude is a retired attorney who has dabbled in writing for as long as he can remember. Yes, he's that insipid eight-year-old who wrote the play for the neighbors.

The Accountant

By Bill Trude

HAVING TO WORK LATE EVERY NIGHT is the bane of many an accountant during tax time. As such, it didn't seem strange to find myself standing alone on the platform of the railroad station of my suburban hideaway as the last train from Chicago departed for points even farther west.

As always, I stood at the crosswalk and watched as the engine slowly pulled the other cars along their allotted path. Since the only way off the platform was on the other side of the tracks, I'd often fantasized about finding myself facing some great unknown once the train had gone. My imagination had taken that fantasy from a homeless bum pleading for money to a ruthless thug wanting the same (but without asking) to a beautiful vestal virgin who wanted to change her condition. Only sometimes did she want money.

But tonight I was very tired. My client had run me ragged, screaming that certain expenditures were certainly business-related, haranguing me for being dumb enough not to see it his way and threatening to fire me for not "just doing it." That's probably why I wasn't thinking of anything except perhaps that the train wasn't leaving fast enough to suit me. And that's why when the train was gone and I actually found myself facing a very real unknown, I was totally lost about what to do. Not that I think any of my imagined offenses or defenses would have done me much good anyway. For one thing, most them involved using my briefcase in some manner, and due to the late hour, I'd left it at the office. And for another, what I was facing wasn't a virgin or a bum or even a thug. I was standing eye to eye with a dog, a very large dog, and, from all appearances, a very angry large dog.

I know my heart skipped a beat because I felt it. I also felt it leap into my throat. I also felt in that instant every other cliché that stands for being scared shitless, except of course for the shitless part because all at once I felt like I needed a bathroom very badly. But there wasn't one or anyplace else to hide for that matter. There was only me and a growling dog or, to be more precise, a growling German Shepherd or Labrador Retriever or Rottweiler or something big and ugly.

It's not that I don't like dogs. I love dogs. But I love them better when they're small and furry and comfortable to be around. When they're large, growling and baring their teeth, I need to get used to them before I can love them. I hoped this dog would give me the chance to get used to it so that I could love it, too.

"Hi, puppy," I muttered through a throat so constricted I wasn't sure anything could get out. "You're a nice puppy, aren't you?"

His deep, dragged-out, throaty "grrrrrrr" said it all. He was no puppy, and he was in no mood to be nice.

I took a step back. I knew it was only a few feet to the eight-foot high chain link fence that guarded the platform from the fifteen-foot drop to the street below. Still, it was better than nothing. Much to my horror, he took the same step. I took another. He did the same. Before I grabbed my option of taking a third, he beat me to it.

Fear was quickly deteriorating into panic. I tried to force myself to look around to see if there were alternatives for my retreat, but I was afraid to take my eyes off him. And he knew it. And worse, he seemed to love it. His dazzling, ghoulish grin was getting wider as centimeter by centimeter his teeth were becoming fangs. I was suddenly positive he'd feasted on human before and was at that moment craving his next morsel.

I felt my shoulder blades hit the fence. I was going no further, at least not backwards. Moving to my right or my left seemed like poor to hopeless alternatives. He'd just follow. My only way out was up. But that meant turning my back on my enemy, and try as I might I couldn't get myself to do that.

That is, until he took the step I was unable to rival. Then I had no choice. So I tried a half-turn, keeping one eye on him while trying to grab the fence with both hands.
It didn't work very well. I only got one hand and no eyes on the fence, but it did serve to remind me of one thing – there was no way I was going to climb in my leather shoes. They were wider than the apertures. I thanked my lucky stars I'd slipped my loafers on that morning.

I concentrated on keeping eye contact with the dog while I got out of my shoes. It did no good. He noticed and took another step in my direction. I figured he was now within lunging distance. I had to move quickly, and without due deliberation, I did. I swung to my right and grabbed the fence as high as I could. I then threw my legs up as well, trying to catch a high foothold.

As luck would have it, I succeeded too well. My hands and my right foot, the only one that stuck, ended up closer than I'd intended, and I had little to no leverage. I was like a monkey hanging from a branch, only not nearly as agile.

I didn't know what to do. Should I pull my knees up to a position where I could free up one hand, or should I risk setting my left foot lower on the fence so I could improve my balance? As I wrestled with this decision, the dog made his move. He growled his fiercest growl and seemed to throw himself against the fence. I couldn't see him, so I wasn't sure whether he was trying to bite me or knock me off. Either way, he failed, but I didn't think he was done.

I was right, and with his next effort, he made his intentions clearer. He was trying to do both, and his range was getting more accurate. While I was able to hold my position and he wasn't able to bite me, he did get hold of my left pant leg.

"Shit!" I muttered as I felt him tugging at what was a very integral part of my $1,000 Armani knock-off. "Why this suit?" I'd only bought it the week before and was wearing it for just the second time. What's worse, I'd worn it purposely to impress a client who hadn't even noticed.

"Come on, doggie," I whined, "be good and let go." I thought he had when I no longer felt pressure on the fabric, but I was wrong. When I went to move my left leg, his grip kept it firmly in place.

Unfortunately, my grip wasn't doing as well. Due to bad weight distribution, the cold metal strands were cutting into my fingers and right toes. I needed to move. Figuring I had no other choice, I yanked my leg harder, but all that gave way was my suit. The slow sound of "rriipp" was a god-awful sound.

"Please let it be in the seam," I whispered as I settled back to consider my options.

It didn't take a genius to figure out I didn't have many. I thought of shouting for help, but I could see from my meshed perch that the small park bordering the train station was deserted and that the downtown stores were dark. That's exactly what was expected at this hour. "Bedroom communities" didn't get that designation by having a swinging midweek nightlife. People were supposed to be home in bed, not hanging on a goddamn fence.

Besides, making a lot of noise didn't make a lot of sense. The saying goes, "let sleeping dogs lie," and, at that moment, the dog wasn't doing anything.

And that's when I realized he wasn't doing anything. He wasn't growling. He wasn't nipping at my heels. He wasn't shaking the fence. What the hell was he doing?

In order to see him, I had to let go with something, but that was kind of a given since all my somethings were going numb. The fingers on my left hand were throbbing the most, so that's where I started. It was painful, at first, to unclench them but it felt indescribably good once I had. As I hung on with only my right foot and hand, I could easily lean back and get a bird's-eye view of my adversary. And there he was, five feet ten and three-quarter inches directly below me, seemingly staring off into space. I looked to see if there was something that caught his interest, but there was nothing.

"What do you want, doggie?" I asked quietly.

He glanced in my direction, but he didn't answer, not that I'd gone crazy enough to think he would. But he just sat there with my pant leg hanging from his mouth. He didn't growl or bark or even bare his teeth. Unlike earlier, he seemed relaxed. In fact, it was almost as though he hardly cared if I was there.

I wondered if he'd already achieved what he wanted, and if he had, what it was. So far he'd succeeded in scaring me to death and had a mouthful of my suit. Neither of those seemed like a logical goal, but then why should they?

"You're dealing with a dog, you idiot!" I inadvertently said too loudly.

That caught his attention. It wasn't hard to tell. His ears moved forward and his nostrils twitched. Besides that, his expression visibly changed. All at once, he looked like he was wondering what I was all about.

"Oh, no, you don't. You're not turning the tables on me," I said as softly but threateningly as I could. "I'm up here because of you. So don't you go giving me that look!"

I should have known my chatter would bring a reaction, and it did. His expression grew even more acute as he cocked his head to the side like Wags used to do.

I told myself to ignore that and not to think such thoughts. This was not Wags, nor was it anything like him. Wags had been my boyhood pet, my chum, and my confederate. This dog had torn my best suit and driven me up a fence. He was an enemy, a brute, a hazard. The only problem was that he suddenly looked so damn adorable.

I realized I was losing my focus. I couldn't afford to do that. It was important that I stay alert. I had to take the offensive.

"What is it you want?" I appealed. "My pants?" I knew that sounded ridiculous, but it was the only thing that came to mind. "Well, you can have them. But only if you let me down."

He cocked his head again. And then, to my absolute shock, he stood up and tried to back away from the fence. Now, he couldn't do it and still hold on to my suit, but I swear to God, he acted like he really wanted to back away, like he wanted to give me room to get down.

I decided I must be losing it. If it wasn't bad enough that I was talking to this dog, I was now thinking I was having a conversation with him.

"Doherty," I said, purposely out loud so I'd be sure to hear, "you're human, he's not. He doesn't know what you're saying." Besides, I knew if he did want me down, it certainly wasn't for my pants. He wanted me down so he could eat me.

But he didn't look like that. Dogs who want to eat people don't wag their tails and start hopping around like Benji. At least, Wags didn't. Wags only did things like that when he was happy to see me. And the more I talked to this dog, the more he was acting like Wags, albeit a larger and more intimidating version; but like him nonetheless.

I decided I had to risk moving. I knew I couldn't stay on the fence till morning. I'd lose feeling throughout my body and pass out before then, and it made sense to get off while the going was good, when the dog was in a good mood. Still, I was going to take it one step at a time.

And that's exactly what I did. I moved a foot; I checked the dog; I moved a hand; I checked the dog; I moved the other hand; I checked the dog.

At first, he seemed to be watching each motion with great interest, but as I got closer to the ground, his attention waned as he again looked off into space. When I finally had both feet back on the platform, he smugly swiveled his gaze upward to mine as if to say, "Well, it's about time."

If he'd been a person, I would have had lots of unpleasant things to say, but under the circumstances, I only muttered, "Okay, I'm here. What do you want?"

He looked me as though it was obvious, and then I realized it was. I'd promised him my pants if he let me down, and he was expecting me to keep my end of the bargain. Before I had my belt undone, however, he started to whine. That was something new, and I didn't know what it meant. By the time I unzipped the zipper, it had turned into a growl, if not a snarl. I stopped what I was doing. He did, too.

"What is it you want?" I moaned. "I'm really tired."

All whimpers are sad, but he suddenly emitted one of the saddest ones I'd ever heard. He couldn't have meant it, but since it seemed the perfect response to my complaint, I decided to interpret it as being sympathetic to my plight. As such, I took the initiative, and with a majestic sweep of my hand toward the stairs I asked, "What do you say we get off this platform?"

You could have knocked me over with a feather when he stood up and took a step in the direction I was pointing. In fact, I was so astounded, I forgot that I had to go with him. It was a rather uncomfortable pull near my crotch and another sickening "rriipp" that reminded me.

"Hold on," I laughed.

He stopped as I quickly reached down, picked up my shoes and hurried to catch up. When I thanked him for waiting, I assumed the little shake of his body meant I was welcome.

Since our dialogue was going so well, I didn't even think when I asked, "Do you have someplace in particular you want to go?"

But this time I'd gone too far. I didn't even get a glance. He just kept walking. With me dutifully following, he plodded across the tracks and over the platform. The stairs proved a little tricky, but he allowed me to stay a step in front so my pants wouldn't rip any further. Since the tear was along the seam and was still below the knee, I hoped the suit was salvageable.

When we reached the wide-open space of the park surrounding the station, the dog suddenly hesitated, did a full 360, and stopped. He looked up at me with a doleful expression that made my heart sink to my shoes. For the first time I was afraid he didn't know where to go, and that was the last thing I wanted.

Since we'd made our acquaintance, I'd been telling myself this was just a dog on the run, away from home, on a lark. Once we started walking, I hoped we'd get near his house, he'd let me go and everything would be fine. True, his lack of identifying tags was an indication I might be wrong, but it was only an indication. He could have slipped them when he got away.

But his not knowing where to go belied that scenario. Worse, it left me in charge, and that was a responsibility I didn't want.

We were doing fine with him leading the way. He was considerate of my feelings, and I was getting to enjoy his company. But I knew if I had to make the decisions that would change. I couldn't afford the luxury of thinking about him the same way, and he could come to regret choosing me for his ... whatever it was he'd chosen me for.

I stood there looking at him for more than a moment, but it didn't take that long for me to realize that my being in control meant taking him one of two places, and one of those didn't make any sense.

It wasn't that I didn't have a home. It's just that it wasn't much of one, and it certainly was no place for a dog this size, particularly one of questionable character. My neighbors' walls abutted mine, and the Homeowners' Association had rules regarding pets. I'd only glanced at them, but I had a feeling my newfound companion violated, at least, the one regarding weight. Besides that, I lived alone and was gone all day.

I tried to tell myself that didn't mean I couldn't take him home for the night. But it did. For one thing, I had an early-morning appointment that I couldn't cancel without screwing up the whole day. But that was an excuse. I knew if I let him into my house for even a minute, I'd end up disappointing both him and me. I couldn't have him thinking he'd found a new home, and I couldn't risk me thinking I'd found a new friend.

I had no choice. I had to take him to the police station. That was the sensible solution. After all, people called the police to report their dogs missing. So naturally that's where people who found dogs should take them. If it proved necessary, they'd also know where the nearest pound was. It was just that simple.

But it wasn't that easy, not nearly that easy. All I could think of was the time when I was a little kid and my friend found a dog. And it was a nice dog. It didn't rip anybody's suit or scare them out of their wits. It was a little bit of a jumper but not that much. Still, when the police couldn't get him into their car, and he struggled with that loop they were trying to get around his neck, they shot him.

I didn't think they had to. Neither did my friend nor his sister nor my father nor my mother nor my friend's mother. But my friend's father and the police said it was necessary. As my eyes met those of my fellow traveler, I heard the blast of a shotgun and saw a small circle of blood on the grass.

"You idiot," I declared with a confidence and smile I didn't feel, "it's not going to come to that. You're not going to let it."

I genuinely smiled when the dog reacted to my declaration by pawing the ground and delivering a resilient snort. Instinctively, I fell to my knee, gently grabbed his neck with my left arm and patted him on the head. "It's not going to come to that. Is it, fella?" He eagerly nuzzled my face with his nose. I loved it. It was just like the old days with Wags.

I quickly forced myself back to reality and reproached myself for taking a trip down memory lane. This wasn't the time for it. I gave the dog one more quick pat and was back on my feet brushing the dirt from my one good pant leg and my other knee.

"Come on, guy, we've got places to go and people to see."

It wasn't even a two-and-a-half-block walk from the train station to City Hall, but it took us almost half an hour. He sniffed every bush and tree in the park and then every parking meter and fire hydrant thereafter. It wasn't that I was in a particular hurry, but his gait was plainly slow, and every effort to speed him up proved futile. It seemed as though his back legs were giving him some difficulty.

About halfway to the station, I stopped to see how he'd react to being touched in the hip area. When he did nothing except wag his tail, I got down jowl to jowl with him and asked if he was all right. I decided his nuzzling my nose wasn't a definitive answer, and perhaps a vet could provide a better one. The problem was where to find one at two o'clock in the morning.

I didn't even try. I thought about it, but I didn't try.

I did hesitate before entering the police station, but only to check to see if the dog sensed where we were going. Again I wasn't sure, but when he displayed no displeasure, I concluded he didn't. Thank heaven for small favors.

The Desk Sergeant, or at least that's who I assumed he was, gave us the once-over as we ambled across the small lobby, but it wasn't until I was standing directly in front of him that he quipped, "You've got a friend."

"So I've noticed," I deadpanned before giving him an abbreviated description of how

I'd come to be in my position.

He appeared to be listening patiently since he waited until I was through before he asked, "And you want me to …?"

I thought it was obvious.

"Act like a policeman."

"Oh," he said with a nod. "Okay. Meaning?"

"Help me with this dog?"

The crooked smile that permeated the lower half of his face was disconcerting. "Help you how?" Before I could give him what I thought were unnecessary suggestions, he added, "If you think I'm going to get between his teeth and your pant leg, you're nuts."

I couldn't blame him for that, but in all other ways, I thought his attitude was less than helpful.

"I was thinking more along the lines of reports of missing dogs."

"We don't have any." He must have noticed my raised eyebrows cause he quickly added, "Believe me, I'd know if we did."

"I see," I said in hope of keeping the lines of communication open, but it didn't work.

He said nothing, absolutely nothing. "Well," I began again with a new approach, "what do you normally do in cases like this?"

If anything, his smile widened. "I've never seen a case like this."

His whimsical approach to my dilemma was wearing paper-thin. "You know what I mean."

He started to laugh. "Yeah, I do … but mister, you don't realize how stupid you look. It looks like the dog's walking you."

He was wrong, I realized. From the moment I walked in the door and saw the look on his face, I realized. But what difference did it make? It didn't change anything. I still needed help. So we – that is, the dog and I – just stood there.

"We take strays to the shelter," he said, finally relenting. "If you want me to, I'll call one of the patrol cars to come and get him."

That's not what I wanted, but I didn't stop him when he picked up the phone. Before I had the chance to reconsider the possibilities or change my mind, he informed me that an officer named Jack Maloney was on his way and would arrive ASAP.

"Does he like dogs?" I asked.

"You got me hanging. Does it make a difference?"

I shook my head, but I didn't mean it. Of course, it made a difference. Otherwise, I wouldn't have asked. But I couldn't admit why. I couldn't stand the thought of appearing any more sappy and foolish than I'd already been made to feel. It would be easiest on all concerned to just allow this escapade to play out.

I was grateful when he let the subject drop and started to rustle around in his desk drawer. I took the opportunity and turned my attention back to the dog. He was doing just fine, but his inquisitive look seemed to beg for an explanation of what was happening. I bent down and patted his head. I hoped that would suffice for the moment.

When the Desk Sergeant stood up and curiously announced, "While we're waiting, I'll get you free," he aroused my interest. The huge pair of scissors he was holding in his hand as he rounded his desk received my full attention.

"What are those for?"

"I'm afraid there's nothing else I can do," he stated flatly. "I think you're gonna have to lose that pant leg."

"No!" I said holding out my hand to stop his advance.

And happily it did. The sudden movement along with my protest had startled the dog. His hackles started to rise and his head turned in the direction of the oncoming scissors. I quickly kneeled down, patted his back and told him everything was fine. Since the last thing I wanted was anyone seeing any semblance of the brute I'd met on the platform, I breathed a sigh of relief when the dog quickly relaxed.

"In that case, you're going to have to lose the pants," the sergeant surmised with an inflection in his voice and an expression on his face that left no doubt he thought it was a weird choice.

"I'd like to go along with Officer Maloney," I stated. His expression grew even more dubious. "I think it would be easier on everyone concerned if I went along. I don't think the dog will give anybody trouble if I'm there."

He put the scissors on the desk.

"It's okay with me if it's okay with him," he said pointing toward the main door. I looked as a patrol car pulled up to the curb. "You're still going to have to get disconnected sometime, though."

I nodded my head.

"We'll worry about that later."

He smiled his crooked smile and wished me luck.

Officer Maloney was younger, trimmer, and a lot less cynical than his office-bound counterpart. Without needing any explanation, he told me he was "glad to have me aboard" because "he wasn't much good with dogs anyway."

Of course, he then went and proved himself a liar by devising the plan that got us into the car. After my unsuccessful attempt to get the dog in first, he suggested I get in the back seat but leave my "leg with dog" on the pavement. He reasoned if I then slowly lifted that leg into the car, the dog would follow. And to a point he was right. The dog managed to get his head and front legs in, but he couldn't lift his back ones high enough to get them over the frame.

We exchanged sad looks before the officer whispered, "I don't want to get bit, so hold on to him and tell him everything's all right while I help him." I did, and we were off.

After another brief explanation of how the dog and I came to be, I asked if there were any chance there'd be a vet at the shelter when we got there. Officer Maloney said he'd only been there once and that was during his orientation.

"But I hear Doc Sulley's a night owl," he added, "and he lives right there. So maybe. We're supposed to wake him if there's an emergency, but I don't think this is an emergency, do you?"

I hated to agree, but since I did, I dejectedly responded, "No."

"I don't think that dog's dangerous," he persisted in a cheery manner. "He's just old."

"Yeah, I guess you're right," I said as I looked down into eyes that suddenly seemed terribly sad. "But he didn't seem that way when I saw him coming at me at the station. He was more like the Hound of the Baskervilles."

From the vacant glance I got from the front seat, I knew he didn't catch my literary allusion, but he must have gotten the general idea.

"It was the circumstances," he said with a chuckle. "You know, it was dark, it was late, there was nobody else around. Hell, an ugly squirrel might have scared you."

An ugly squirrel! I laughed but didn't object. After all, he had a point. It probably was the circumstances, and maybe I had been partly responsible. Maybe my actions had led to the dog's reactions instead of vice versa. It made sense.

"Maybe I overreacted a little," I confessed.

"Oh, I didn't mean that," he protested as he turned off the road and parked next to the only other car in a small parking lot. "You gotta be careful with animals. They can be dangerous. That's why they surrounded this place with a fence."

Indeed they had, and a very high, unattractive fence at that. But that had clearly been a blessing for the neighborhood since the building was even less attractive. It looked a great deal more like a miniature prison than a kindly shelter.

"This is it?"

"It's the place, all right, Alcatraz East. According to my chief, no animal has ever escaped from here except in a pine box." My expression must have reflected my despair. Officer Maloney's ruddy complexion turned ashen as his eyes went from looking at me to looking at the dog. At the same time his right hand reached slowly over the seat and stroked the animal's head.

"Only kidding, pooch. I'm only kidding."

It was an admirable try, but it didn't work. I knew he wasn't kidding. He was right. Most animals didn't leave these places. I knew that. Hell, everybody knew that. I'd been consciously avoiding thinking about it, but, thanks to Officer Maloney's offhand remark, I could avoid it no longer.

I leaned forward.

"Can you go in first and see if that vet is there?" I whispered so as not to upset the dog.

Maloney nodded with an understanding that left me feeling vulnerable.

"Sure."

Left alone again with the dog, my hands started to shake. I felt like I was mainlining ice water, and my stomach was getting more nauseous by the second. I was sure my fast food dinner would soon be making a return trip. What's worse, the dog wasn't cooperating. He began whining and pacing around the small back seat all the while pulling at my pant leg. I wanted to yell, "cut it out," but I knew it wasn't his fault. He was agitated only because he sensed something was wrong, and he was right.

I needed air, and I needed out of the car. I threw open the door, but before I could move the dog was all over me trying to beat me to it. I grabbed on to him so he wouldn't pull too hard. He growled but didn't try to bite. I held on.

"It's all right, guy," I murmured. "It's all right. I'm going to get out, too."

Thankfully, he calmed down just enough for me to make the first move. I put my left foot on the ground and carefully helped him follow. I was afraid he'd try to move away from the car, but he didn't. He waited for me to get out and then looked up as if to ask, "Where to now?"

Just the thought of the answer left me lightheaded. I leaned against the car, shut my eyes, and took several deep breaths, but I didn't want to focus. It was like my body and my mind were running separately, and neither wanted to be in the moment. I felt a little crazy. Tears were welling up in my eyes and a rage was mounting in my belly.

It never made it out. Somehow Officer Maloney's cry of, "He's here" managed to break through my semiconscious stupor and pull me together enough to look in the right direction. I saw him standing in the doorway, and when our eyes connected, he yelled, "Come on, the Doc's waiting for you."

I nodded confidently, but I didn't think there was any way I could move. I was wrong. Gradually one foot did follow the other, and I was walking. I didn't bother to look to see if the dog was following. I didn't have to. Where else would he be?

"Believe it or not," Maloney exclaimed as he led us through a dank hallway to the small consultation room, "Sergeant Rudly called ahead to say we were coming. Some people are really hard to read. Know what I mean? I never thought that old fart would lift a finger to help anybody."

For some reason, I wasn't as surprised, but I wasn't up to debating the point. For one thing, I still felt more than a little wobbly, and, for another, my mind was on other things, like the fact that we were actually in the shelter.

No, that wasn't right. It was no shelter. Shelter meant safety. Shelter meant refuge. This wasn't even close. The antiseptic smell, the concrete gray walls, even the glaring fluorescent lights screamed "pound." I didn't need to see cages or needles to know what this place was all about.

In fact, I decided I didn't need to see anything more. All I wanted to do was get out of there with the dog. But I didn't get the chance. Before I could think retreat, Officer Maloney had me by the arm and was introducing me to an elderly gentleman with a very firm grip.

"This is Dr. Sulley."

I tried to smile.

"How do you do."

"From what I understand," he replied as his eyes perused our situation, "probably a lot better than you. I hear you've had kind of a rough evening."

I nodded and thought about asking for his guarantee that it wouldn't get any rougher. Instead I just mumbled, "The last couple of hours could have been better."

He laughed sympathetically as he went down on one knee and playfully ruffled the dog's neck. "Have you been giving …" He stopped and looked at me. "I'm sorry, I didn't catch your name?"

"Brad Doherty."

He smiled at me as though he thought it was a nice name before he turned his full attention back to the dog.

"Have you been giving Brad here a tough time?" The dog wagged his tail just a little. "Well, that's not very nice, is it? He seems like a perfectly fine chap to me. Don't you think so?" The dog responded with a slight shake of his head. "Yeah, I thought you did." He let the dog nuzzle his face before he stood up.

"I can tell you he's old. But if you want to know any more than that, I'm going to have to examine him."

I totally misunderstood his intentions.

"I'll pay."

"No, it's not a question of that. In this case, I'm just like Officer Maloney here. I'm working for the city. I just meant," he continued as he gracefully swept his hand from the dog's position on the floor to the top of the examining table, "how do you want to handle this? I mean, can we get him up here like this? Will he let you go?"

Since I wasn't sure about that, I suggested we try to get him up while he and I were still attached. At first, it worked like a charm. Between our three calming voices and gentle touches, we had him lying on his side on the table without a hitch. But that was only temporary. It soon became clear the doctor didn't have suitable access to his patient with me running interference.

One by one we tried to coax the dog into letting go of my pant leg. We each met with equal lack of success. "I could sedate him," Dr. Sulley suggested. "That would probably relax his jaw enough so we could get it out."

I shook my head. I knew sedation would relax more than just his jaw. It would relax his other muscles too. That suggested complications, and complications were something I wasn't prepared for and we didn't need, at least not yet.

"Then I don't think I have a choice," he stated as he grabbed his sharpest instrument and indicated the place he intended to cut the material.

Before he could touch anything, I was taking off my pants. "But I do."

My fellow humans smiled indulgently as I gave them my best embarrassed grin and said, by way of explanation, "His head doesn't look comfortable that way anyway. I figure if you can fold these up and make a pillow."

"That's a great idea," Dr. Sulley stated gently as he took my pants in hand. "I'm sorry I didn't think of it myself."

At first, I stood watch as the doctor conducted his examination. But when it became obvious the dog wasn't going to misbehave and watching became a constant reminder of what was at stake, Officer Maloney and I adjourned to a nearby room that served as makeshift cafeteria.

"Want coffee?" he asked. I nodded and went to get my wallet from my pocket, but it wasn't there – the pocket, that is. "I got it," he said without even a hint of sarcasm.

"You're getting kind of fond of that dog, aren't you?" he continued. When I answered by way of looking down at my bare knees, he added, "We've been told to discourage that in the case of strays. You don't know where they've come from. Lots of them have been abused, and that can lead to violent behavior."

I knew he was just doing his job, but I didn't want to hear any of what he was saying. Still, that was my problem, and I shouldn't discourage him from doing what was probably right under most circumstances. I said nothing.

As he handed me the coffee, he put his hand on my shoulder and took the seat beside me. I fully expected him to continue in the same vein. When instead, he said, "You don't want to hear any of this shit, do you?" it came as a relief. I shook my head. "Good, cause I don't want to hear any of it, either."

After several seconds of a not-uncomfortable coffee-sipping silence, he asked if I was married. When I shook my head, he said he had been for eight years. Since we were about the same age, I figured he must have gotten married at the time I was starting my career and working on my MBA.

His wife was a dental hygienist, and they had a four-year-old daughter named Caitlan with another baby on the way. He was hoping it would be a boy, but he'd told his wife it didn't matter. They were renting a small house in town but were diligently saving for a down payment.

"But it's going to take forever," he said with a smile. "Prices are so damn high in this town."

He asked if I owned my home. I nodded and told him I had one of the two bedroom condos near the train station. It seemed he'd looked at them and liked them, but "they're too expensive and too small for my family."

He said he loved his job but not his hours. It was hard on his family life, "although it saves on babysitters." He went on to tell me he'd been assured by the chief that he'd be getting better hours soon.

"It'll seem strange sleeping at night again."

He asked me if I liked my job. I told him I'd always been good with numbers, and it paid the bills.

"I'd say from the looks of that suit," he said with a playful poke to my ribs, "it pays some world-class bills."

I was grateful someone had finally noticed, but I didn't respond.

On weekends, he played in the various police and fire department sports leagues. "You know, football in the fall and basketball in the winter, baseball and golf during the spring and summer. Besides keeping me in shape, it's a lot of fun, and my wife says it keeps me out of trouble. What could be better?"

When he asked me what I did for fun, I told him I went out now and then, mainly with people I met at work or the health club, but as far as dating, there was no one special. Otherwise I liked to read and watch movies.

"Oh, and I play golf now and then."

His ears perked up just like the dog's had.

"Where?"

When I mentioned the name of a prestigious local private country club, he was impressed. When I explained I could afford it because my company paid the bills, he was even more impressed.

"Wow, am I in the wrong profession or what?" he joked. "Seems to me like you've got the world by the balls!"

I couldn't help but smile. I'd never thought of it quite that way.

It was while Jack, as he insisted I call him, was talking handicaps, the golf kind, that Dr. Sulley called me back into his office. Despite my invitation, Jack thought it would better if he stayed outside "for the moment." I told him I thought that's all the time it would take me.

As I walked into the room, I knew the news wasn't good. It's time to beware when a doctor puts on his professional demeanor, and Dr. Sulley was certainly wearing his. He'd donned a white coat, and the grave expression on his face mirrored that of any viable candidate for "Funeral Director of the Year." Knowing what I was about to hear, I found myself trying to picture the situation as a Charles Addams cartoon. It still wasn't funny.

"I'm sorry to say," he started somberly, "this dog is very ill. He's got tumors running throughout his body. Some of them I can feel by just touching him." He paused as though waiting for me to say or ask something, but I could think of nothing.

"While he doesn't exhibit any pain, he has to have some. That's what's causing him trouble with his back legs." Again he waited. So did I.

"Beyond that, he's definitely blind in one eye, almost completely deaf and, while I haven't had the chance to examine his throat, I don't think he can swallow properly."
I'd heard enough.

"So you're saying...?"

Now it was my turn to wait. It was only after a suitably reverent interval and a visibly deep breath that Dr. Sulley responded, "I guess I'm saying that, if he were my dog, I'd help him pass."

While that's exactly what I was expecting him to say, that wasn't how I expected him to phrase it. For that reason, it took a moment for me to give my prepared response.

"He's not my dog."

Dr. Sulley's expression changed instantly. He clearly no longer felt the need to look grim. In fact, he smiled as he gently patted the dog whose head was still resting on my pants.

"I think he'd disagree."

That wasn't what I expected him to say. It wasn't even close to what I expected him to say. From his appearance and what I'd seen of his disposition, I was positive Dr. Sulley was going to be nice about it. I was sure he was going to say that he understood and that I should go home and that he'd deal with it. I'd even rehearsed my exit. I was going to say "thank you" and "there's no way I can tell you how much I appreciate your help." Then I was going to get Officer Maloney, or as I should say, Jack, and run like hell. But now none of that seemed appropriate. Instead I just stood there.

"I don't mean to be difficult," he continued in a voice barely above a murmur as he gingerly held the pant leg protruding from the dog's mouth, "but, you see, he thinks he's still holding on to you. And I can't get him to let go."

I tried not to, but I couldn't help it. I had to walk over and see for myself. It was true. The dog's jaw was as firm as ever.

"What do you want me to do?" I asked.

Dr. Sulley gave me a nonjudgmental shake of the head.

"It's not what I want you to do. It's what he wants you to do."

At first I thought he must be kidding, but the look on his face broadcast sincerity. I felt ill again. I didn't know what to do.

To make matters worse, when I asked for guidance, the doctor only shrugged and said, "I haven't the foggiest idea. Ask him, I guess."

And that's what I did, but only after I got down on my knees so I could look him in the face.

"Hey, fellow, how ya doin'?" From the gleam in his eyes, I knew he could hear me. "The Doc here tells me that you got some problems. Seems like you're pretty sick...like maybe you're in a lot of pain." I patted him on the head. "Are you in pain? Are you?"

For a moment, it seemed as though he might turn a little so he could sit up. But then he didn't, or couldn't. I wasn't sure.

"That's okay, boy, just stay the way you are. You're doin' fine."

I glanced up at the doctor. Without saying a word, he gave me the impression I was doing the same – fine.

"The doctor says you got lots of tumors. But you probably already know that, don't you, fellow?" He nuzzled his nose closer to my face. "Yeah, of course you do. I mean, you know if you don't feel good. Right?" I was stalling because I didn't want to get to the hard part. I ran my finger down his nose. "The problem is he says there's not a whole lot we can do for you. He's already done all he can. He can't make you any better."

I looked for a reaction, but there was none. I looked at Dr. Sulley. He looked sympathetic but said nothing. It was all up to me. I slowed my breathing and stared intently into the dog's eyes. With all my heart, I willed him to understand.

"What the Doc here and I got to know is ... if you feel up to going on." I knew that wasn't good enough, not by a long shot. "What we got to know is ... if you want to keep on living."

There, that did it. My heart began to race and right along with it went my mind and speech.

"Now, if you do, we'll work it out. I don't know exactly how yet, but if you do, we'll find a way. Maybe, if you promise to be quiet, it could even be my place. Matter of fact, if you promised to be real quiet, I know it could be my place. So if you feel up to it, we'll make it … together … a team."

My babbling had begun to excite him. He again tried to get off of his side and into a position where he could stand up. But this time there was no doubt. He couldn't.

"But if you don't feel up to it," I slobbered while ferociously petting his stomach, "that's okay too. We'll understand. We all know how tough it must be to be in such pain. So if you don't feel you can, we'll understand, won't we, Doc?"

I looked up. Dr. Sulley was nodding.

"And the Doc can help you. He's allowed to. He's allowed to help you so that you have no more pain. He's allowed to help so you won't feel anything bad. He's allowed …"

I was exhausted – exhausted and terrified. I felt like I should stop, like I should wait and catch my breath, like I should think about what I was saying. But I couldn't. If I did I knew I'd never finish. And it suddenly seemed monumentally important that I finish.

I readjusted my position to ease the pressure on my knees and refocused my gaze with that of the dog.

"You understand, don't you, fella?" His eyes were cloudy but not vacant. "Yeah, I know you do. I know you understand." I reached out and cradled his head in my hands.

"So, guy, I need you to help me." I leaned forward and whispered in his ear, "I need you to let me know what you want." I closed my eyes and rested my chin next to his. I waited, for only heaven knew what.

And I suppose, in one way or another, that's exactly what I got. Within seconds, my face was being bathed in what we humans like to classify or, better yet, misclassify as dog kisses. But these weren't the kind they like to show in dog food commercials, the kind where the puppy is passionately slurping all over some guy's face. No, these were unhurried and protracted caresses, dispensed with a tenderness that literally pleaded, "be kind." When I opened my eyes, I wasn't at all surprised to find that slightly chewed piece of my pant leg now lying on the table.

Dr. Sulley explained that there'd be two shots; the first was a sedative to allow the dog to sleep and the second was a much stronger one that put him to sleep. He asked that I stay through the first. Jack, who'd reentered the room at some point without my noticing, told him we'd be there for both. I didn't argue.

I like to think it was because I was sitting holding him in my lap when he got the first injection that he exhibited no fear or discomfort. That's bullshit, but I like to think it anyway. As he was falling asleep, we each said our good-byes. I have to give Dr. Sulley credit. It was a first for Jack and me, and the Doc was a good sport for playing along with my foolishness.

When, after the second shot, I was told his remains would be cremated along with several other animals, they both looked at me as though expecting me to ask for some ashes. I didn't. That would have been stupid. Scattering his ashes on the platform would have been for my benefit, and I already knew there was no way I'd ever watch another train depart my station without thinking about what had just happened.

On my quiet ride home in the patrol car, I looked down and noticed a few stray hairs clinging to my left pant leg. I bent down to pick them off and fought the lump rising in my throat. Jack looked across the seat and smiled reassuringly.

"Would you like to play golf at the Club sometime?" I asked impulsively.

"That would be nice."

I nodded in agreement as I delicately placed what I'd just salvaged into my jacket pocket.

For information or to purchase copies, go to
amazon.com or contact:

University Club of Chicago Writing Society
76 E. Monroe Street
Chicago, Illinois 60603
312.726.2840
ucwritingsociety@gmail.com

Made in the USA
Monee, IL
18 December 2019

19101818R00098